Copyright © 2023 Evie Campbell

EVIE CAMPBELL

A READER'S TALE, BOOK 3

A reader's tale.

Copyright © 2023 Evie Campbell.

Copyright © Genevieve L. Hughes, writing as Evie Campbell.

Cover overlay photography irises, and original vectors ©GLH
Fonts used under license with Canva.
Shakespeare's quotes and epigraphs from Romeo and Juliet, and Hamlet, are duly recognized via notations.

This book is cataloged with the National Library of Australia.

A catalogue record for this book is available from the National Library of Australia

Paperback ISBN: 9798386633813

Dedication

To the Indie readers who bear witness daily to Romance-landia's perverse sense of reality, and survive to read. To those who bowed and scraped. Who were abused and screwed over—for the love of words, in support of authors. That's a novel in itself. *You are worth so much more. Walk away and never look back.*

To the authors who've spent years refining their craft. Their profession and brand–despite plagiarism, bullying, abuse, and concept theft. You remain humble—you're the real deal. You're worthy of the crown.

Lastly—to the authors who rose as bloggers, ARC readers, and personal assistants—riding on coattails and borrowed words. Do you think your numbers count—your theft and corruption are the only way? You're so damn wrong. We've already forgotten your names. Enjoy the wake in your honor.

The Smut Mafia and their influencers—crushed.
Their litigious methods—exposed.
Their leader—ghosted.

Thou shalt not speak.
Thine lips are sealed.
Pray for forgiveness for remaining silent.

We broke our oath.
We joined their ranks.
It's always been the bottom dollar.

Those who filled the abyss,
Were fueled by a deadly desire,
To RiZe above the corruption.

Non content Warning

We don't do those here, they're detrimental to the plot; if you really can't live without them turn the page. This satirical parody mocks Indie publishing/promotion; it is not factual, nor is it a how-to book. Liberties were taken.

Brief terms for reference—this is not book padding or a scam, terminology may be found in the glossary.

Please research unfamiliar words via your ebook lookup (Web/dictionary). Readers are smart; don't underestimate them.

The author is Australian, so please forgive them for any unfamiliar phrases used.

An FYI: the author adores and utilizes em dashes extensively, because this is how she was taught to write.

Content Warning

Warnings for: Online bullying, mental health, off-screen self-harm. No cheating (except book boyfriends). Slow-burn, dual POV with flashbacks. If timelines and diaries jar your sensibilities, skip this read.

This novella contains adult content and situations. It is not suitable for persons under the age of 18 years.

Prologue

Past

RiZe of the team

In the spring of 2017, seven gathered at a popular diner in the deep south. A faded, blackboard menu listed greasy, fried food, from flapjacks to has. The twenty-four-hour service ensured the place was busy. Like so many remnants of the past, its black and white checkered floor, red vinyl booths, and low lighting, suited the agenda to perfection. No one would remember the venue–no one would recall the patrons. It masked their devious behavior and long disregard for rules.

Established as social media bloggers—a tight-knit community—the team desired a crown. Not by serving their time, but by making quick bank. They'd identified a loophole. No ability or hard work was required—moreover, no one would notice.

Between rounds of drinks, their ideas combined, nourished by calories and sugar, the final components of a conspiracy came to fruition. Spread before them, mapped out with sticky notes, sugar shakers weighed down a battle plan—a get-rich-quick scheme—to be hidden in plain sight.

Their agenda bordered on perfection in its simplicity and finesse. Its execution, like most hyped novels—appeared successful, yet failed dismally under scrutiny. To succeed, an army of minions was required—young readers desperate for books to fill empty places in impressionable lives.

The Smut Mafia established themselves with no outlay—a group of stay-at-home moms and bored, cash-strapped college students. Offering minimal representation, only the ignorant could fathom was fine–they covered minorities, and excluded diversity.

They weren't readers, authors, or artists. Future professions were covered—an up-and-coming law student, a teacher, an English major—sufficient knowledge was pooled to provide feasibility. It wasn't done for the greater good, but merely an untapped resource, begging to be taken. The con–steal, establish, hype–*and never, ever back down.*

They began their push—burned it down—and succeeded, above all expectation, to the shock of all. How did an obscure group of nobodies, rise to power? To reside in the ivory tower of Indie, and reap rewards in the form of traditional contracts?

You'll not find proof of their meeting now. Perhaps a few photos remain on personal pages, who knows? Those young women are long gone. Faces altered cosmetically, or with filters, they became their book characters—corrupted by a power struggle to stay on top of a crumbling kingdom.

We watch their desperation daily, their rise to fame, elevating the corrupt with them. If you serve them well, you might be offered a slice of the cake.

Cross them, and we know how it ends in Romancelandia.

Tell me, how did we let it go this far?

Chapter One

Present

Authorgate

Read. Write. Review.

Set against the salacious backdrop of independently published romance novels—women wronged women–victimizing their own. Author versus author–they tore into each other—further dividing unstable factions.

Until they ripped one too many.

They'd created a kingdom built on broken promises, crushed bones, and dreams of others. Words stolen in the dark depths of night—prose was taken hostage, claimed as their own—yet not of their making. The literature they purportedly wrote was far beyond their comprehension and intellectual age, or ability. It was clear to anyone with a smidgen of intelligence. When asked about inspiration or characters, they'd claim to have moved on, or, *'I can't remember, it was so long ago'*, fell from bloodied tongues, their halos slipping. You do not forget your children—your book babies. If they'd only realized the content stolen was about them—not for them…

Called out anonymously, the worst of the worst—the guilty—erupted. A prehistoric oil spill—black, rancid, and tar-like—boiled to the surface. They flooded every aspect, every group, screaming *their* outrage. They were *complicit* in plagiarism, yet *denied* accountability.

Their vicious intent exposed—without source or early access—they fell with the velocity of a crippled aircraft. The impact detonated a string of events so brutal, it scorched the air we breathed, leaving dust in their wake.

The Smut Mafia forced hard-working men and women into a corner. There was no coming back from reader and author outrage. No coming back from the fallout of their actions—so we thought.

Biting the hand who feeds you is never advisable. Publicly destroying them—the rise of the mean girls—without follow through, what's the point? It's repetitive and boring—we've witnessed it time and time again. The same spoiled children who abused categories utilized loopholes, and raked in cash—their little bubble burst, leaving them to fend for themselves. Their target missing, they sought alternate routes to circumvent wrong-doings.

Small author cliques jumped on the bandwagon. They repeatedly denied allegiance, yet were privately supporting the problem—generating free promo, new options, and ultimately, income.

They became complacent in the belief they'd won. Bored and beyond reproach, a vocal campaign began on an author's page—a *cinéma vérité* unfolded, in full view of all—they bemoaned their circumstances and fall from grace. Included in the tirade, assistants-turned-designer, come-author—no holds barred, vicious—they became braver, toxic, and dangerous.

To add further insult, to their continuous injury against the reading community, charities connected to them via anthologies.

The opposition, mid-feud, in turn, jumped on the cause band-wagon, for visibility and an attempt at a worthless title. After all, if you can't obtain one on your own merits, hitch a free ride on the reader's sympathies.

Emulating rabid dogs, they roamed in packs, attacking authors, readers, and artists alike. With no regard or conscience for their actions—being *authors, sensitive creators, after all*, it was their *right*. A frenzy of hatred fueled them and ignited; the inferno blazed out of control. Their true colors flew, and flags fluttered in the turbulence. Until they fell silent.

As the light dimmed, and the fire smoldered, there were no apologies or acts of contrition. Their appalling behavior was de-leted—feeds cleansed of hatred and anger. The self-loathing, vile, and ugly inner selves they'd aired to all—their outward beauty could no longer conceal, disappeared.

Devout readers and followers who'd *abandoned* them were re-placed by causes and *fake* good deeds. To mask their true nature, voices rose in support of world events, communities, and political actions. Not out of the goodness of their hearts, but all in the name of furthering their careers.

Visible briefly, they'd move quickly on to more aesthetically pleasing events—no one questioned funds raised—nor were they made publicly available. You'd assume a large donation in a singu-lar name created amazing tax advantages.

New devotees replaced the old–unknowing of the risk or gossip. After all, the majority of the community refused to sink so low as to raise their voices against one another. They'd never contem-plate social suicide by doing so. Most stepped away graciously, with the maturity you'd expect of professional businesswomen. Some understood and could not intervene, others were in the dark, only having heard rumors. The few with first-hand experi-ence *said nothing*—were they complicit, or threatened?

Below the new veneer, hatred continued to brew and spread. It was time to reinvent–transform a dying scheme, into something new and shiny.

Distraction was always the key.

The thieves were rewarded for their efforts with stolen awards, boutique contracts, and independent movie deals. In the meantime, their second string rose, in case of fatalities. Debuts, and baby authors, appeared from the rubble–too well known if anyone paid attention, with high follower counts and connections. The content of the *new creators* was too polished and overly familiar. It was not virginal work—this was their backup plan.

The Smut Mafia did what they do best–recycled. The consequences and lives destroyed, be damned.

But what if I told you a new puppet master sat front and center the whole show? If I told you the end of their reader deception and vast publishing creation was almost nigh? Would you stick around to hear the story?

Chapter Two

All the world will be in love with night - Romeo & Juliet

The Maestro sat at the crossroads and lured them, alluding to promises of grandeur, fame, and fortune.

Readers came from the south to the call of a siren of old. Bloggers moved in from the west, desperate for a piece of notoriety. Narrators blew wind from the east, hesitant to get too close—fearful of losing control. Authors sat high on their northern throne, in the belief they were protected and invincible.

Amid the chaos, and convergence—safe in his snow globe—the Maestro sang sweet lyrics.

Words the authors wrote down to replicate—in awe of his talent.
Words the narrators begged to voice.
Words, both readers and bloggers, obsessed over.

They'd all sell their souls for stories and blindly follow the piper. None understood the intrinsic value or true purpose of the Maestro. The pressure to perform, maintain momentum and direct a new regime–epoch-making.

This was the breaking point—the boy with his finger in the dyke, collapsed under pressure. It was always the intent to drag the conspirators from the shadows, but he underestimated the cost. Attention spans waivered, and the thrill of the hunt subsided. The Maestro who'd gently directed and fed them sweet nothings, walked away unnoticed—and vanished.

Waiting at the crossroads, as equals, desperate for their next fix—stood the hierarchy of Indie. Exposed to all, its mask shattered—all that remained were shards of carnival glass and a river of crocodile tears.

Lost without direction, without a guiding voice, decisions, and reckoning–were left to the masses—the readers. To hold those accountable for their fraudulence–and play judge and jury was overwhelming. Ultimate justice for all, or continued favoritism of a select, plastic few?

Chapter Three

Past

Kat

Smut_Mafia_Official - Thursday 10th December

Rhett: Wanna play cat and mouse anyone? Bada boom! PMSL. Like that @Kat?

Mina: You crack me up every time @Rhett. We've not played to-gether for so long. Wink, wink.

Rhett: Not *that* kind of cat lol. I have an idea. This a new twist on an old fav just between us girls for now.

Kat: Funny @Rhett. It's not like I haven't heard it before. I'm in, but no more song lyrics. I can't deal with another knockoff. Those cheesy eighties, one-hit wonders passed off as prose, gag. They'll be the death of me.

L.B: YES @Rhett!!! You're finally finishing the trilogy? Praise the book gods. About fucking time. What's it been, almost three years?

Rhett: Yes and no @L.B., it remains a duet, sorry girl. Lyrics? You do know readers aren't intelligent enough, to understand what they're reading. It's why including cheesy, over-the-top song lines, remains the go-to. No one reading the books recognizes lines. Until they're caught out, who's going to call the copyright police? Anyway, who remembers my first time around?

@Gloria, @L.B. and @Mina, add wave emojis.

Gloria: Sure do. You tanked lol. *'No one's changing my words. You don't understand what they mean to me.'* Hell, you were such a whiny, baby author. Always explaining your story. Differentiating between show and tell remains your worst habit.

L.B: Don't forget 'I *really* appreciate your input and advice, but...' PMSL you were so fucking arrogant to Rani @Rhett. No wonder she dumped your ass.

Rhett: Thanks for the reminder @L.B. Business is business. As Dee so kindly opened her trap and shouted the name I buried to the world, I had a thought. Why not use Lyla Day? Let the old me out. No one's around now to silence my voice.

Mina: Isn't it still a secret? Dee will lose her shit over it. You hid it for years, so why now?

L.B: The old you didn't hold back, but fuck it waffled on. PMSL

Gloria: What did we expect when the 'author' refused to accept edits?

Rhett: Not that voice @LB, you twat. My *author's voice.* And yes @Gloria, *now* I listen. So, the plan is, I'll steal @Kat away from Caz for a bit and rework Lyra and Xavier again. There's more than sufficient work for the plot group for months, so Kat's services are better utilized with me.

Mina: Dee'll love you forever. She's waited for this and the dedication you promised her.

Rhett: Yeah, possibly not. I'm turning her around, swapping Lyra and Xavier out for Lyndon and Xavier.

Gloria: Now, there's a great idea. The trope is an easy sell. Look at everyone bragging about their banners. They're cheesy as fuck, and in the children and young adult listings PMSL. Of course, they're going to score there with underaged teens.

Kat: By swapping out, do you mean changing the title and cover out? Haven't you unpublished and retired the pen name?

Gloria: No, Kat. I think Rhett's trying something you'll enjoy. As for the pen name, Josie's bloody anthologies still have the original. She can't bury it deep enough.

Rhett: Ladies.

A cover mock-up hits the chat. We're hit with a clean-cut, drop-dead gorgeous blue-eyed blond. His legs wrap the low slung, leather-clad hips of his partner. Tattoos encase both men—a snake slides around cut abs, mirroring the other. Supported by one arm —guns ripped and beautifully defined—the second guy grabs his throat and tilts the blond's head back. Pure sexual tension emanates from them. Lyndon, by Lyla Day, in sapphire blue topography, with the tagline *'Bend or break, I made the darkness my friend.'*

Gloria: Fuck me sideways. Dee's going to lose her shit over this one.

Kat: True art. Stunning cover, Rhett. Congrats. The photographer captured the moment beautifully. It's sheer perfection.

Rhett: Wait until you see the teaser photos. You'll get your panties wet all over again. It's time for exclusives. The market's ripe for the trope. If Amy can add a top ten with her twelve-year-old writing style using one of my plot concepts, mine's easily number one.

How can we not agree, as smileys and gifs fill the page? It's a brilliant idea, not honest, but it's how they roll.

Rhett: So, ladies, are you available? One of our team found a beauty to insert and beef up this baby. A few tweaks and paragraph drops—a little editing help and voice change, easy. Lyndon's a dead-set bestseller. Meet me in private @Kat I need a few minutes to brief you.

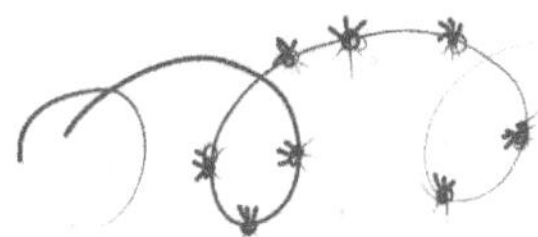

Rhett & Kat's_$_Chat

Rhett: Hey, hon. I know Caz has you running ragged, but this one's easy. Sierra already went over it, and the outline's dark and gritty. Minimal edits are required, so you're the perfect fit.

Kat: How many words? Time frame? I'm not reading for anyone—you know my rules. I won't edit the same trope between reads, just in case.

Rhett: I do, but it's only in my favor. I can't have an alpha or editor inserting *similar* words or phrase suggestions into others, can we?

Kat: So, you said something about the perfect piece? Is it legit? I'm not putting anyone at risk. Please tell me it's better than Lyra.

Rhett: Hell no, this is old work—I think I was fourteen or fifteen when they pushed me to publish Lyra. It's absolute rubbish. But the contemporary lot thinks they're reading something dark and erotic. They'd piss themselves if they opened up the real deal.

Kat: No, I've read Lyra's book. I know Dee wanted it tidied up. Something about you promised her side character a book and a thank you.

Rhett: Don't tell her, but I finished it twelve months ago. It keeps her hanging on. As for her *dedication*—she contributed by sharing the blurb. She may have posted on her blogs and hyped posts–and I paid her for each promotion.

Kat: What's this injection of words? You've reworked it, and it's a quick edit?

Rhett: This one's a cut and paste. They found an obscure piece dated 2014. It's poetic, the same year Jada disappeared. Odd, but anyhow. Lots of choice sentences we can copy and filter through. But dumb them down a little–they're a touch snobby. Readers don't care much if they have to think too hard about it. Sheep need simple words and a few toys to satisfy those carnal urges.

Kat: I'm confused. You're reworking, right?

Rhett: Sure, I'm swapping male/female with a touch of heat. Turning it into a full-blown male-on-male storyline.

Kat: Just swapping out the FMC for a guy?

Rhett: No one will notice. We'll just turn the FMC into a twink– they have the same effeminate speech pattern and actions. Add some glitter. Sickly-sweet puppy dog eye crap. Dark nails, a little makeup.

Kat: I don't think it's that simple, Rhett. Guys speak and react differently to women. Try reading a male author's LGBTQ work. It has a distinctly different feel.

Rhett: Sure it does. They think with their cock, and it feels cheap. Nothing beats a female author's POV when it comes to writing smut. Look at the Breakdown series. Amy's hitting banners with it. My words, inserting her cheesy meet-cute high school writing style. An idiot can write this now. Grab any writing software, and let it fill in the blanks.

Kat: I honestly can't stomach the series. I don't understand its success. The plot outline is fun, but.

Rhett: Of course it is. My work's always great. No, I take that back. It's fucking fantastic.

Kat: Easy then. Polish the original, unpublished work. Change out the female lead, and make it a male, correct? One of your early works, right?

Rhett: Then slide in a few choice sentences from the other doc.

Kat: I still don't get this unpublishing stuff. Why not just leave the books live and rework them online? At least get a little income in.

Rhett: Too much fucking around updating errors or content. I get Nola to format mine anyway, so it's not as simple as correcting whatever the whiny bitches report. I just pull them, and when it's time to move on, a little gloss, a few borrowed quotes, and it's all new again.

Kat: It's all legit, right? I keep seeing posts about piracy and plagiarism online. Please tell me these are your updates.

Rhett: PMSL, you keep asking me that. Sure they are–whatever you want to call them. One of my *early works,* if it makes you feel better? No one looks close enough. They're too busy getting off on the smut to worry about comparing notes. Everyone does it–this is how Indie works. You'll catch on soon enough.

It's hard to pick up sarcasm in chats. I should have paid more attention to the overall tone. The scam was in front of my face and escalating the whole damn time. Looking through notes months later, I still can't believe how gullible I was.

Did I stay, despite Evie, begging me to leave? Of course, I did. The temptation to dig into their scheme, pull it apart and understand– a drug—an addiction. It was their hook, after all. Break down how someone thinks, push their buttons, allay fears, and provide sustenance and support. Create the family they require–superficially, at least–and milk them for all they're worth.

It was their game—my end game became entirely different from theirs. The team may have instigated the battle but didn't foresee the outcome.

Chapter Four

Past

Kat

Go wisely and slowly. - Romeo & Juliet.

I studied the rats in their natural environment, tempting them with peanut butter and cheese. They swallowed the bait every time.

Paying close attention to tropes–their behavior was difficult to decipher initially. I knew they were going about their business–promoting seemingly legitimate talent and connections. All the while, the industry appeared oblivious—readers certainly read to the point of ignorance.

Upcoming trends to push were easily predicted simply by the lineup in the plot documents. MMA, Bratva, meet-cute. Next, it would roll over to Motorcycle Club and combinations. Add a little suspense, crude, hard characters—television impersonations of the fake underworld, and the releases were coming thick and fast.

To make matters harder–some bright spark declared teenagers were the next in thing–high school age, bad boys. Remember the movies from the nineties? Instead of down-on-their-luck, leather-wearing trailer park kids—they were multimillionaire, alcoholic, drug abusers. They owned fast cars, faster girls, and controlled insanely ridiculous situations.

Something changed overnight, in mid-2019. Inexplicably, Mafia appeared on their radar—more importantly, mafia princesses and human trafficking. The game altered, along with the market. Captive reading was popular.

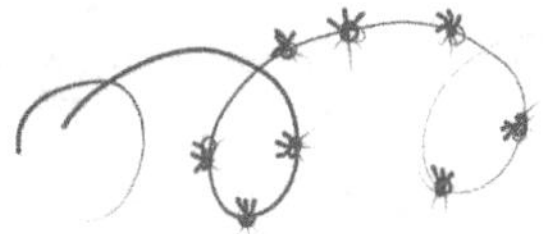

Past - Smut_Mafia_Official 7:30a.m., December 18th

D.D.: Happy fucking Monday, skanks and sinners. New game, new rules, we're moving house. I've sent private messages and links to those who've made the team.

Group members lit up the chat as they logged in, one by one. Dee's week-long absence, and unceremonious return, set off gossip.

Noticeably, Caz was missing.

D.D.: Drop whatever you're doing. Those with invites have two hours to swap sites. Your link's invalid once I lock the group. Everyone else, sayonara, thanks for your past support.

D.D. left the conversation.

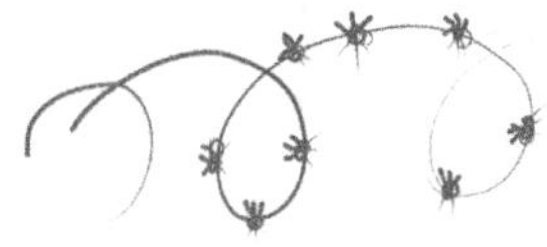

www.Book_Martyr_Server

Book_Martyr_Chat 8:30 a.m., December 18th

D.D.: Welcome ladies. You may bow to your queen now you've made the last cut. Note I'm having Alyse drop this into the swag. You'll find it in the online store, *Dee's_the_fucking_queen.*

L.B: What about the rest, Dee?

D.D.: The rest? If they make it, fine. If they get lost along the way, their loss. Welcome to our new Book_Martyr_Chat team. The new server's connected to the back end of the plot team and author support services.

Kat: Now it's connected to the business? What happened to you doing it all for love @D.D.?

D.D.: Love doesn't pay the bills, hon. Not all of us have sugar daddies who leave us to play.

Gloria: yo, book whores. FML, the link wouldn't sign me in. I thought I'd miss out.

Chat fell into a familiar rhythm and catch-up. Dee's reappearance was readily accepted and nothing unusual. New candy dispersed–it was all they cared about.

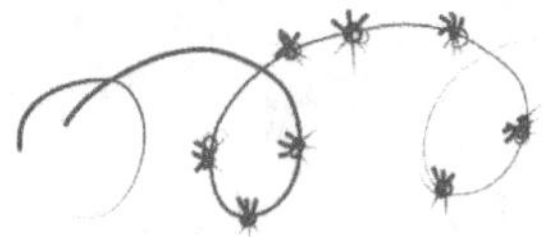

Two hours later

Kat: Hey @everyone. I have a question about an upcoming release. Each time I follow the author's link, the book price has too many zeros.

L.B.: Author and title? I'll see if I have the same issue.

Kat: Amy's latest, the MMA one. You know, the cute pink, artsy cover?

D.D.: Don't bother looking. I'll save you the time @L.B.

L.B.: She didn't? Tell me she wasn't stupid enough to sign up for it. Here we go with another boxgate episode.

D.D.: Of course she was. I warned her, but *I know fuck all*, as you know.

Kat: I'm missing out on something here. Does someone want to fill me in, please?

D.D.: Stupid bitch signed up for a book box.

Kat: Exciting! Tell me where.

L.B.: Sorry to burst your bubble @Kat, but the wait list is insane. My guess is the cover's going to be exclusive to the box.

Kat: She posted release info on her page. How can it be an exclusive and a waitlist? She's not a big name, so they'll have stock, won't they?

L.B.: Nope. They'll tie her up with the *limited edition* cover. Any spare books left over, readers will on-sell. At a premium for the box, of course, pretending they purchased them.

Kat: What about her fans? Why limit to one supplier? They'd have hundreds available.

L.B.: Try limited to no more than one hundred. Depending on how tight finances are, possibly as low as fifty. She wants to be a white elephant author.

D.D.: Unicorn author, you twat, @L.B. She wants to be a unicorn.

L.B.: It could be worse. Imagine wanting to be something fluffy.

At least an elephant has a good-sized trunk lol.

D.D.: Sparkles and glitter are more her style. The bitch has too many teeth to be a cute fluffy pet.

Kat: Guess that's me missing out again.

L.B.: I'll send you a link to the resale group. Be warned, ten-dollar books end up costing a couple of hundred.

Kat: What the actual fuck?

D.D.: Don't get her started @Kat. @L.B. hates the BookBargain-Whores Group.

L.B.: They profiteer. The bitches who run the group, the boxes, don't get me started on how they rip off every person involved.

Kat: Hmm, gossip? It sounds interesting. How do I find these groups?

D.D.: Oh hell no, you don't. We don't touch those crazy bitches. Stay in your lane and avoid them at all costs. First and only warning, you will be burned by them.

L.B.: They'll eat you for dinner @Kat, just like everyone before.

Kat: More gossip then? How bad can it be? I did a quick check on their tags, top tier authors there. Covers are out of date, like, way out of date. Something weird's going on with the matte crap too. But if it tickles something for them.

L.B.: Their author access is only possible because of introductions. Like all the other bitchy bloggers in her clique, she used the fuck out of me. Avoid her, I'm warning you. The flakey, dyed-blonde, sweet-as-pie, stay-at-home mom gig's fraudulent. She's one of the most manipulative pieces of work out there.

D.D.: You tell her @L.B. Or maybe not PMSL. Don't get her ranting about how screwed over she was I beg you @Kat. Better yet, ask Evie. She did her a few favors along the way. Reading some of the chat screenshots, the woman is as crazy as fuck, and vicious doesn't begin to explain her.

L.B.: Just avoid the bitch. She's threatened litigation against half of the Indie population at one point. Off her rocker is being complimentary.

D.D.: As for the matte covers, they allow bloggers to print paper copies and cover old books. They pretend they have a physical copy of the book, so the advertising's hidden as a book-related post from data searches.

Kat: What the fuck is wrong with you people?

D.D.: As if we can afford to buy the books we read. Just fake it til you make it.

Kat: But authors conspiring, setting their covers to aid and abet fake posts?

D.D.: Do you honestly believe authors bother to purchase copies of their books? Most can't afford the rent, let alone waste money on paperbacks.

Kat: Who came p with the brilliant fake book photo idea?

L.B.: The same one selling backdrops and flat lays, Rhett.

D.D.: Don't let her claims of being inept at social media fool you. She's a genius when it comes down to dropping things in and covering her ass.

Chapter Five

Present

Kat

Conspiracy theories

"I opened a novel by an author I admired last week. Imagine my utmost surprise to discover the words were familiar—words I'd written as part of another's outline."

The disgust on Damon's face was mirrored in his tone. "What type of author requires another's words, thoughts, or life experiences to write?"

"None. They're not authors if they do. They're certainly not creators, just mimicking what others do."

"Outlines and prompts are potentially helpful, surely?"

I'm so over the facade these women promote daily. Having to explain it over again to Damon doesn't ease the headache pounding behind my eyes. "It goes deeper, so much deeper. They're liars. Every aspect of their professional life is a fallacy. It's become so ingrained, the belief system so screwed, they can't help but continue to steal."

"No. If you lack the imagination to create your world, characters, and storyline, fuck! They're not legitimate in any shape or form. Those prompts aren't for would-be fakes to run with–it's for AI."

"Not possible." I'd considered it, but to endorse a system to replace them made no sense. Though perhaps it did, with even less energy expenditure if a computer is generating their manuscript.

"It's the only feasible explanation for the decline in independent publishing quality. If readers can't discern—possibly due to lack of education—the difference between solid content and prose—none of it is real."

"You're suggesting machines are ripping manuscripts?" The abject horror in his voice at the thought matches my shock.

"No, no. People are ripping and feeding them into artificially created novels. Think about the lack of true emotion. The variance in style. Either the author is illiterate, or it's a software-generated output."

"If you're right, how do the remaining few protect themselves? If computers are capable of creating, where does plagiarism end?."

"They're not. Software is mixing words, fed in by the lowest life forms within the community. It also explains review repetition and the lack of critique or comprehension of anything above an eighth-grade level."

Damon's chuckle sends a shiver down my spine, contrary to the topic. "Harsh, Kat. Some are just stay-at-home moms."

"I'm referring to the software. For now, it's incapable of performing the level of intricacies an educated person can. Think about contractions and word choice, for example. Punctuation's another red flag. They're still grabbing source material from multiple documents online."

"Potentially why there's a crossover between tropes and infeasible actions in so many cases lately. Explains the increase in copyright breaches. AI remains unregulated, without morals."

Random sex scenes in a new release flash through my mind. Additional limbs and actions requiring a trapeze artist's flexibility highlighted the author's lack of experience. "Monster porn's one I read. But the need to sketch sexual positions while reading, to work out who should have been in which hole, cracks me up. I guess they've not inputted the Karma Sutra yet."

The sketches reminded me of the caricature cards in a book box flat lay yesterday. Stock photos, fed into AI software, generated gaudy images for sale. Combinations of Rembrandt and classic artworks were evident in the brush strokes and color palette.

"Consider the book box scenario. It's an amazing opportunity for little-known authors to sign up for boxes and promote their work." I remember my first box excitement–immediately extinguished after discovering the process.

Despite the surprise public announcement excitement about book inclusions, readers don't realize how contributions to boxes work with most. It's an application system rather than an invitation, particularly the lower-level entries.

Damon kept several manga-style boxes from a traditionally published paranormal author on display. "It's great for those without the funds to advertise, but they screw over every source to line their pockets and cut coats. Signup forms are available all year round. Others head hunt marketable names without even reading them."

"Pre-release scheduled books with big names are expected. Pitfalls are obvious, regardless of an author's standing, it's easier to upload and over-price the new book cover, ordering direct from a major retailer."

"We see them all the time. A three hundred dollars plus listing for a cover appears for seven days on a retail distributor's listing. It's a red flag, you know a book box has an upcoming release. When the book is only country-specific, we can guess the destination easily. Next, the cover is unpublished, and it becomes exclusive."

"So the box pays the higher rate?"

"Heavens no. The small ones, it's author print cost only. That's another scam in itself. The author receives nothing out of the little mom-and-pop setups."

"They're marketed as special editions aren't they? Exclusive to a particular business?"

"Supposedly. The content remains the same, hopefully. Too often it's not. They pretty up the interior for some editions, depending on the markup and accessibility to free labor. The gutters are off and the page bleed is messed up. Too bad the copies are unreadable, should the purchaser want to read the books."

"You've got to be exaggerating a little. It does take skill to format physical copies correctly. They can't mess things up, can they?" Damon's disbelief is sadly amusing. He should know better by now.

"All at cost, don't forget. Favors for friends, no *training* or *experience* required."

Damon

"Hold on a moment. An author willingly hands a raw manuscript to an unknown person to reformat and control?" Once again, their disregard for rules and for protecting their work stuns me. "Remember the exclusivity clause?"

"Exclusivity does not apply to paperbacks," Kat snaps back, rubbing her temples.

"So these aren't paperbacks you order through any reputable publisher or printer with security measures in place?"

"No, they're boutique boxes. Pop-up businesses without a brick-and-mortar storefront or business plan. Most are fly-by-night, name changes, with multiple business registrations if they're registered."

"Exactly how many in the last few years have you witnessed the collapse and failure of?" The idea astounds me. The idiocracy of supposedly intelligent women continues to surprise me.

"To be honest, until you, I'd paid little attention to the disorganized chaos of Indie outside of the immediate threats." She pauses for a moment, "would twenty surprise you? There are probably a lot more."

"Twenty people or twenty businesses? They'd be registered, contracted, and vetted with the usual privacy requirements. Twenty seems like a high failure rate for a niche item."

"The well-established, reliable sources have been around for years. Never doubt their credibility–theirs are quality-controlled collectibles. I'm talking about authors and their teams after a quick dollar."

"Authors hand their brand, their raw books, to whom? Random strangers?" I'm appalled by the lack of quality control and security in place.

"Apparently. I'm not interested in the whole breakdown of how or why. It's the legitimate access to their manuscript–in a raw form–someone else can reformat, of concern. There's your risk factor. A lot running them are newer authors themselves. How tempting is it to grab raw words and *borrow* them?"

"No one would be foolish enough to risk their work. If it's altered, or heaven forbid, portions of books disappear?"

"They would, and they do. Trace them back and connect dots to the plot thieves or pirate blogs."

"Why the hell don't they look into it? Common sense should dictate protecting your content at all costs." The audacity to scream piracy. This, and ARC reads, add to the issue daily, shocks me.

"Fame. Most crave special-edition covers. Bloggers want to be seen in feeds to plaster their walls with the latest. It doesn't matter if the cover's remotely similar to the characters. No one cares if they're screwed up using pretty, unlicensed imagery. Authors want the street credibility of adding a book box to their resume. No matter how inconspicuous or cheap the product looks, they want in."

"Covers be damned. What are they thinking by handing over malleable work? How easy is it to strip and rework from a document?"

"You tell me. Watch the lineups and quick releases. Search the content. Manuscripts must be submitted months in advance, allowing printing time. If the formatter ghostwrites or edits, what's a sentence or paragraph between friends? I've read books with chapters altered. I'd hesitate a guess it's when they cut and past for themselves–the new content crosses between documents erroneously."

"I don't doubt you, but I'm amazed it occurs."

"Again, reputable companies exist. They do so because of their expertise, in-house printing, and original designs. But—not everyone is created equal. The long-term legalities over incorrect licensing are a potential nightmare, without the theft aspect."

"I don't understand how anyone hands over their income, their own business for others to benefit from their work."

Chapter Six

As with readers, some–not all–authors are addicted differently. They require the spotlight for whatever childhood inadequacies and untreated illnesses ate at them from within. The fragile claims of artistry tend to be more like classic cases of narcissism.

Addicts don't have the mental capacity to consider the consequences of their actions. Narcissists won't admit they're at fault.

Addicts certainly don't want to understand the process of manufacturing a substance—in our case, reading material.

The creators of the game themselves are addicted. The thrill of the chase, how far you can push someone–or something until burned—they tested boundaries on every level.

Addicted readers only recognize the same taste and sensation certain connotations and combinations provide. The endorphin rush of a romance novel, the thrill of suspense in derivatives of the criminal underworld—craved like no other substance.

They're provided with words—words they beg for-minutes after completing their first rush—the intoxication is palpable. Their dealer is already uploading the next artificial fix. In some ways, readers and their fanatical behavior nurture the thrill those stealing words require.

You'd assume our drug of choice is a consistent quality. Why would anyone settle for takeout when there's a five-star restaurant for free? Fast-release, appealing covers and content pander to our demands as requested. Anyone could mistakenly believe it's a fire sale. Considering writing's an art form, why does no one question how the mass production of words eventuates?

Readers are greedy, demanding, and unappreciative. They recognize the familiar feeling—the rush—regardless of the author. The euphoria within a tight-knit group—is guaranteed to fulfill imaginations and gratify urges and needs. Ensuring a leash stays on their readers, similar books–kindly supplied by their besties–are suggested between releases.

Unlike sex or chemicals, words provide an immediate rush–if you find the right combination.

What we don't dare ask or consider is the source. How are hundreds of thousands of words handed on a literary platter from authors younger than some readers' children? How is it even feasible? Most can't string two grammatically correct sentences together online. So how do they churn out dozens of books and story compilations at twenty?

The source isn't the pretty camera-ready image you all see. The origin is many—they are legion. And in turn, the Smut Mafia continues its daily attacks on unwitting writers and gullible readers.

While the source continues to provide sustenance, they milk them dry. It was their coup d'état—discovering prolific authors, forcibly hiding their books in vaulted categories—*they stole the words.* They fed you lies, and you continue to feed *their* habit.

We're all addicts in some fashion.

We need to break the cycle of corruption. We need to stop, look and listen before it's too late. We need to take back control–or it was all for nothing.

Chapter Seven

Present

JD Publishing - phone conference WIP discussion.

Those who rush stumble and fall - Romeo & Juliet

Safely ensconced in their sheltered homes, Generation Z discovered reading and the wonders of Indie. Bored teens and adults flooded social media, searching for entertainment. A celebratory moment for most young minds–broadening their horizons in a secure environment in this day and age is crucial. Indie book sales skyrocketed. The average newbie author, hoping to make a few dollars, was turning over a terrifying $25k a month. Others were hitting millions in page reads. Proudly displaying street credibility they encouraged besties to join them in their endeavors.

Self-imposed and manufactured threats and drama ensued. Conspiracy theories created notoriety—with it came fortune. Piss poor excuses for literature became bestsellers. No one dared look too deeply at the actual words—stolen song lines, movie quotes, obscure literature—other authors' content.

For a few, not gratified by their fame and income, it became an agenda of hatred fueled by ignorance—readers and authors were equally guilty.

Indie created their secluded world. Authors rarely intend to push into traditionally published avenues, content to exist with their manufactured fan bases. Heaven forbid they stepped into the ranks with real competition outside their control.

Readers who delved into the traditionally published sandpit-shunned for not supporting the idea—Indie genuinely required assistance. You must choose one or the other.

How could authors face bookshelves in libraries or stores when they'd ripped the words from legitimate works? LGBTQ is nothing new. Inclusive books have been available since the beginning of time. Theft from traditional books, twisted by manipulative women, created the new banned books brigade.

Indie's not new, either. The current convoluted version, controversial as they are, has yet to submit anything unique to the literary community. Hidden elements of genius were bastardized by greedy writers. Now they profit from stealing words.

Call them out. Ask how and where their concepts arose. It's not hard to connect their devices and reading to established works.

You'd require the assistance of the distributor and irrefutable proof to instigate an investigation. When work is already widely known, despite being subpar, you can't undo it. You can't undo their Indie created-for-television production companies either. Look closely at those. Check dates and productions, then connect the dots.

It remains the conspiracy and control aspect. Their ability to continually manipulate and reinvent–and forgive their sins—appalling as it is—will never change.

The root of all evil remains the bottom dollar.

Why do you think they establish an in-depth relationship between covers, graphics, personal assistants, and reading teams? Now they've *drawn in the media and thrown cash into shell companies. They were all established when they began this farce.*

It's a pyramid effect. Control the sheep–control the flow of words, visibility, book sales, and information. Now they push Indie to a new level, making them visible to a non-reading audience–glued to their television screens.

So begins our latest study on cancel culture. The target—anyone in a novel who does not match their ideal or likeness.

Damon: *It may rub some the wrong way.*

Kat: *First, they need to notice it. Second, do I care?*

Damon: *No, you've made it clear. You're not concerned with what they think. I'm not sure what you'll accomplish. If someone with power reads it–things may change. But not in our lifetime–or that of most legitimate authors.*

Kat: *A single author sitting for twelve hours a day writing can't compete with the sheer volume of exposure fake Indie teams generate. Everyone learns at some stage. What's safe to share, post, graphic sources, licensing, tags, it goes on. Who's a legit business, a hard-working author, editor, blogger, and who's a scammer, with no regard for anything other than taking your hard-earned money? We learn daily who cares little for others and see dollar signs in everything they do— everything has a price or a title. If they can't post or participate, you can't, so act like kids in a sandbox.*

Damon: *This is where we hope crackdowns will stabilize the industry and market. Their use of teams–creating noise and promotion–to over-shadow legitimate works will decline. If they have to pay for their hype girls advertising posts, numbers will decline.*

Kat: *Fingers crossed, but don't hold your breath too soon–the hybrids are out in force. They believe if they can slink in and reinvent social media accounts, they'll be safe. It's still undisclosed advertising.*

Damon: *You realize this is not the way to make friends or influence* *people, right?*

Damon snorts into the phone, stifling a chuckle.

Damon: *Your next author in the making.*

Kat: *I'm not interested in making friends with the scum on an amoeba. And yes, potential new authors, more than likely, alter egos with secondary accounts.*

Damon: *Bloggers.*

His voice breaks, on a deep-chested laugh.

Damon: *There's your favorite word.*

Kat: *If only you understood how insanely predictable they are and how easily they're led along. If you've read this, try that—comparing quality work with cheap knockoffs. God, how I hate those posts. As if actual best sellers, not the category-level banner crap, would endorse a comparison and permit them to use their covers.*

Damon: *They do the same with reviews. If you like, whoever, or referencing characters and worlds.*

Kat: *This! So much this. You can't compare cheap wine with champagne. How do you beat them?*

Damon: *Air some dirty laundry online? Most retain their decency and self-respect. It becomes absent the moment sane and sensible people step into independent publishing.*

Kat: *Most thrive on gossip, requiring it to breathe and function daily.*

Damon: *But gossip is a funny thing. The gossip mongers don't know you personally.*

Kat: *Another life lesson—a speed bump you hit. You pick yourself up and keep going. I'll never warn anyone again about the pitfalls and consequences of this situation. Those involved understand who they're in bed with and irrecoverably turn a blind eye.*

Damon: *Do they simply lack something vital in their daily lives?*

Kat: *You'd assume so. Time tracked on apps, to be seen online became insane during this time. The only thing keeping us from a reset—a new game—was the lack of momentum.*

Damon: *Fighting against a rising tide is almost impossible.*

Kat: *You go with the flow, even if the path is destructive. Join them.*

Damon: *And you prayed for it to improve, even when it didn't.*

Kat: *If you're just along for the ride, as torrents of water rip through lives, you're not responsible. As a storm becomes a tsunami and it hits a land mass, you're not responsible.*

Damon: *Every moment counts. Every droplet of water and a breath of air all contribute to the greater good—or in their case—evil.*

Kat: *But how do you stop a deluge? Is it as simple as pulling the plug? Empty the dam, allow it to dry up, and the flow ceases.*

Damon: *Perhaps. Remove their life source. Water's required by everyone–without it, how will they continue to thrive?*

Kat: *They'll find a way, always have, always will.*

Chapter Eight

Past

Kat

One pain is lessened by another's anguish - Romeo & Juliet

The day my life changed began as most did, touching base with the team, checking chats, and talking up books. Evie's reaction to my questions about Dee the day before–leaving our chat–was a little over the top, but she took everything to heart.

The first push of the day was a new promo and upcoming release. I adored the author, but the cover was unusual, far removed from her usual style. No designer was listed on the promotional material, and the title felt familiar.

With a vague synopsis, I hit up the usual suspects, tag-teamed, and tracked the rest of the team. They joined my prompts, commented, and pushed the post visibility. I returned the favor by engaging and gushing over an unread book. It left a bitter taste in my mouth, a reminder of how fake hype is. It could be an attack on another author, the story someone else's—yet we blindly shared, regardless.

Searching for the title on distributor sites, a feeling of unease washed over me. I kept returning to the blurb. It felt like an old friend, the style reminded me of a project I'd read.

Evie may remember.

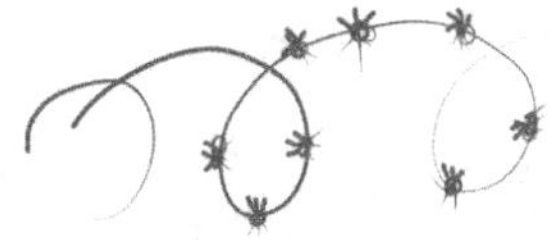

K&E's_book_smut chat. 10:40 am Tuesday, December 19th.

Kat: Hey babe. Just checking in. Thought you may have resurfaced last night and at least said hi.

Evie: Not staying online, sorry. I have so much to clear out today.

Kat: Did you see the posts for Marla Mark's new book?

Evie: I did, what of it?

Kat: I have a gut feeling it's off. I can't pinpoint where, but I've read the words before. Nothing comes up on search strings, but...

Evie: Leave it alone Kat. You don't want in it. Get as far away from them as you can.

Kat: We're not going through this same paranoid chat again. You've been out four months now. I thought you'd come back or gave up on the grand conspiracy idea.

Evie: I'm begging you one last time. *Please,* Kat, walk away from them.

Kat: I just need to dig a little further. It won't be much longer. I promise.

Evie: You have no idea how much is at risk. Extricate yourself *now*, Kat.

Kat: Just this last tour, ok? There's something about this book, but I need a copy. Then, I promise I'm out.

Evie: Leave the book, Kat. It's not worth your life. I'm not joking. They are playing for keeps and don't care who's in the crossfire.

Kat: You've turned into a conspiracy nut, hon.

Evie: Don't say I didn't warn you, Kat. I'm gone, sorry. I honestly have so much to sort through today. I am sorry.

Kat: Fine, go and sulk, Evie. I'm swapping out to their server. Let's chat later.

Evie: Evie left the conversation.

Chapter Nine

Present

Kat

J.D Publishing

Don't judge a book

"**H**onestly Damon, they'll sell you the moon and stars, with the belief your cover must fit their narrative perfectly." He had to raise graphics amongst the plagiarized book titles, today of all days. "My head's pounding from lack of sleep and you want me to remember where I saw the cover?"

Dropping water and a couple of pain relievers beside the glass, Damon runs his fingers lightly over my shoulders. Dimming the lights with the remote, he slides his laptop around to me. "Exclusive, overused, fake posed models, pretending to be teenagers, backdropped by textured concrete. The same style repeats across every photo, with little imagination hidden behind the shutter." The disdain in his voice and hatred of the romance genre gets under my skin this morning.

Clothing and poses—hundreds of shots taken on any day. Hundreds of images are edited and prepared for sale. There's nothing exclusive about the same model, with the same style, on every book cover. Unfortunately, I have to agree with him. "How many authors believe they must have an exclusive cover to succeed?"

"We don't see it traditionally. It appears to be an Indie promoted idea."

"Back to our original group and their *rules*. Ensuring they profit every step of the way through publishing." I detest the system they've ingrained in every new author. The tens of thousands they believe are required to succeed.

"Another percentage and kickback. What's the going rate of a single photo?"

"The classier, professional photographers, pose with brand names, or stonewashed denim and leather. Five o'clock shadows, perfectly honed bodies, hair, and features—all wasted art forms on smutty content. Potentially one thousand upward." I flick through his cover examples and proudly click on two of my favorite photographers.

"Look at the overall lack of balance. The typography is off, sorry Kat. It's tired and cliche." His tone is non-committal, almost abrasive. "Once genre and trope specific, gone are those days. The established, old-school designers fail to refresh their training or seek further experience outside of their favored trope. Show me your choices then."

"Photographers range from backroom hacks, using their garage floors, to world travelers and billboard-worthy talents." I search for more to back up my evidence. I know some appear cheesy, but there are some fantastic examples of artistry. "The hacks–you'll find are the most expensive. Just be sure they know how to license the work. Nine times out of ten, it's not confidential. It's all over the internet before you've revealed yours."

I uncover a portfolio of an unknown author. The stark black and white photos are pure magic—stunning in their simplicity. I don't recognize the models, but the photographer's talent is undeniable. "See!" I spin the screen back to him. It's become a side-show-alley game. "This is how you do it. No one can misinterpret them as anything but romance."

The screen fills with shots of toned flesh, muscles, and tattoos. Beauty personified in the statues created in stills–forever immortalized in film. Middle to perhaps upper thirties, the men aren't over-posed—emotion screams from the covers.

"Holy fuck. I can't believe she published." I track the synopsis in the pre-order. I remember her name in my feed last week, commenting on another post. She was bragging she's now published in multiple tropes as a male/female and male/male author. She was supporting one of her *team* who'd also moved into the trope, reducing its credibility back to poor quality, homophobic-laced drivel.

"Who? The look on your face is classic and terrifying at the same time. Who's upended your world?" Slamming the offending laptop closed, I'm spun into the warmth of Damon's embrace.

"Rhett's back. I honestly thought she knew better and was gone for good." My mood plummets further, knowing what comes next. "So much for no money for covers. I knew they'd do deals to get back in the game, but the outlay, she's about to push hard."

"Very little you can do, Kat. If she's ready to go, you know there's a fast-release series headed our way."

Trembling, I know a series will be the least of my worries. "I need to tell Sara and Zan before they discover this themselves."

Chapter Ten

Present

Kat

Sara's - You have to throw in a surprise

"Friday night carbs and sugar. I can't remember the last time we were together." Zan props her feet into Sara's lap, stretching out on the sectional.

Running her finger along the arch of Zan's foot, Sara watches the toes wiggle. She ceases abruptly, her expression vague. "What's the latest gos, Kat?" Waving her fingers at Damon, lounging beside me. "Are you two a thing now?"

Damon's chest vibrates beneath my fingers as I play with his buttons. "Are we a *thing*, Kat?" His mirth echoes Zan's childish reference.

"I guess we are. I hadn't put a label on *this* yet. It's still new."

"For over a year? Hate to tell you, babe–it's not new." Sara's glowing, and it hits me.

"I think you have news for us S. This impromptu carb loading wasn't accidental." I take in her glass of soda, "neither is refraining from alcohol."

A look of pure bliss lights her face clutching Zan's fingers. She drops a quick peck to her lips. "We have news. I didn't want to say anything so close to Evie's birthday. Perhaps it's meant to be?" A grin envelopes her face morphing into a full-blown smile. Tears pool in her eyes. "We're pregnant."

Sofa diving, I wrap my arms around my best friend and lifeline. "You're going to be amazing moms."

Zan rubs her fingers over my shoulder, "we want you to be her godmother."

"Her? You know already?" My hand slides to Sara's stomach, like every other person who invades a pregnant woman's space. It's instinctive. It's as if we can feel the burgeoning life. The slight bulge beneath my fingers, disguised by her tye-dyed pants. "How far along are you, Sara?"

"Sixteen weeks. We wanted to be sure after the last time–before we made grandiose plans."

"Yes, of course, I will. I'm honored. Congratulations to both of you. I can't believe you kept this quiet for months."

"We didn't want to impose. We knew how busy you were, attempting to establish new relationships with reputable authors."

"Hardly an imposition. I can't believe you'd think that. So what's the baby's name?"

"It's a mouthful. I hope you're ok with it. Elizabeth Katherine Carole-Smythe." Sara runs a finger down my cheek, wiping happy tears.

"Evie would be honored, as am I."

Any thought of warning them about Rhett's series will need to wait.

Chapter Eleven

Present

Kat

J.D Publishing

The remains of our brunch litter the desk. Egg rolls in oil-stained boxes, paper towels, and chopsticks, are in desperate need of the bin.

The ongoing discussion, over reader ignorance, is a tragedy in itself.

"Shakespearian tragedy wise, consider Romeo and Juliet, it's a tale anyone who's read comprehends."

"Of course. Compulsory reading tends to ensure they do." Damon's clean freak comes out of hiding. He begins picking up the leftovers and bagging them up.

"The Smut Mafia reminds me of Juliet, and her *'where for art thou Romeo?'*"

He leans over and refills my water glass. "In what way? You're referring to authors versus scams and plagiarism still?"

"Thank you." Our greasy meal possibly wasn't the best choice so early in the day, I'd rather curl up on the chaise and nap. "Of course I am. The legitimate author's the one on the balcony calling for her reviews and book sales, as she bemoans Romeo's absence. Romeo's been the thief the whole time, not of her heart but her words."

"Interesting analogy. I'm unsure many would choose that particular tragedy. There are so many other writers and works to compare to."

"This remains my favorite piece because they always were fated to destroy each other. All their youth and beauty were stripped away by conflict and misdirection. Outside forces and combatants left them without a choice." My love of Shakespeare and analogies sparks my motivation again.

"Factions make sense. Divide and conquer and no one will cross the demarcation line to compare notes and create a strategy. Instead, we lose everything."

"There are no legitimate winners. Good doesn't overcome evil, how many cheesy quotes would you like? Those who understand the rules win. Anyone who pokes or stabs at them in any way disappears. Simple."

"I'll take your Romeo and Juliet, and raise you with another memorable quote—*To be, or not to be: that is the question.*

"Hamlet's soliloquy. Perfect."

I glance up at the framed array of covers Damon has edited over the years. "The cover topic, sex sells, I thought more on it last night." I'd mulled over it well into the early hours. The combination of plagiarized material, cover control, and every aspect mimics traditional deals in a most corrupt fashion.

"As a profession, it's one of the oldest. There will always be a need, in the same manner, we require doctors and lawyers. How they've abused it for literature, is not the best move. It's set the industry's credibility backward. Pushing boundaries places targets on books, and encourages banning. Not by distributors, but politically."

Sexy covers do sell, the memory invokes a giggle, reminding me of a misspent youth and my poor stepbrother, in a house full of women. "As a teen, I remember Sammy, someone. She wore lace panties and a leather bra—spread across my younger brother's wall. A plastic caricature in a disposable world. Hidden under his bed was a collection of torn magazines and paper towels. My mother cursed him throughout his teenage years—deviant, disgusting—cruel words fell freely from her bitter mouth." My throat's parched, and I grab another quick swig of water, draining the glass.

"I may or may admit to a similar poster. Mine was a blonde in a red bathing suit with an oiled chest beside her." Laugh lines crease the corners of his eyes. "Now, we have social media and gorgeous cover models, with women who openly display self-care items. Nothing better than ads for butt plugs and vibes on your feed. The slips of vag and nipples in photos are never accidental. Filtered or not, there's worse they'll be exposed to daily by influencers—book porn if you will. Openly marketing sexual opportunities under the guise of reading."

"Heaven forbid the romance warriors hear you call it *book porn*." Hell, now I'm calling it book porn. They'll hang me on the mast beside him too.

"We both know they extend their explicit percentage well beyond reasonable inclusion. They're trying to avoid the dungeon and erotica tags. It's not romance, but soft porn, on a good day."

Damon's response to an issue I've deviated from brings me back to the present. "I wonder how Dale's dealing with our boys. They're going through the same process and age of self-discovery. I fear for them. There's little I can do."

A subtle shake of his head reminds me it's a no-go topic when we're working.

"Answer me this. When did we cut ourselves off from human contact and relationships, expecting a girl blatantly selling herself, and a book, to satisfy our basic needs?"

"Mid-pandemic maybe? Readers have always read—now it's a competition to see how immoral or depraved they can behave online. *Authors*, I'll use the title lightly, one-up each other, but forget writing's a craft."

"Preachy much? I know you're not, but I understand the frustration, day in, day out."

"I didn't sign up for slutty sales spiels, filling my feed, hiding my friend's posts, that's for sure."

"World-weary, maybe?" Damon's grin conflicts with our gender references. "I prefer the hot man-chest covers they're holding. Don't forget, they're teens–overly influenced babies."

"Who allows a fourteen-year-old to read those depths of filth and graphic acts unfiltered? Mom or Dad buys them books, so they can pose in lingerie, promoting the equivalent quality of a dollar store book. They adore the authors they promote—then reenact scenes online."

"You're well aware of who. It comes back to the question of accountability. What kind of adult intentionally chooses category listings children have access to? Circumventing social media groups, some members are twelve to fourteen-year-olds. "

"One with no care for anything other than the dollar and a banner."

"Loopholes again. I hope when their kids behave this way—when they're engaging in exhibitionism and deviant sexual acts, as preteens, destroying their self-esteem—they remember the generation they influenced."

"Watch the Prima Donnas drop screenshots of their disgust at the practice." My mind goes back to authorgate and the screenshot nightmare it became. "I'm betting many still have evidence of their actions."

"They can deny and rant all they want. Whose decision was it to begin a war against women? The lying and cheating have to cease. Authors support authors—I call bullshit. It's not a lifelong fraternity pledge. No one's legitimately supporting another who's making bank while they wait their turn in line."

"Always two-faced, nice as pie, until it hits home. Happy enough to make a name for themselves, and attempt to clean up their image after the fact when it does."

"Screenshots don't lie, and you'll find a way to remind the book world."

"The rest haven't succeeded. The decline into oblivion continues. Trends push harder invalidating legitimate works."

"Too often we're lost in trendy things and forget reality. Readers avoid classics and genres outside of their favorites. Back to basics and grounding, I think too many have forgotten how to read. I'm well aware the Smut Mafia don't know how to write."

When did it become so complicated? Books line my walls–tomes of great works, established and new authors, classics beside manga–all cohabit shelves in synchronicity. They don't argue about who sits with them.

"Stress-free relaxation was a promo book in my feed last week. That's a joke. Reading was one of the most pleasurable experiences, now opening a book's become a chore." As a reader, the pressure to review has always been on my mind. The competition to add book counts to sites, regardless of status–I'll remain a reader. "I can't remember the last book I finished. The thought of reading creates anxiety. Not reading leaves a feeling of failure—I'm letting them win."

Damon leans in closer, "It's fear-driven, fine. What's your biggest fear right now if you find a new book?"

I mull over the question, considering why I ceased devouring books like the candy they are. "Will it be real? Is the content truly the author's work? Am I supporting a thief or offering a critique of a real talent?"

Damon drops his pen and twists my fingers with his over the desk. "You're meant to be a reader first. Always. Then a writer if you so choose. It should be a pleasure to create, not stressful or destructive. You know how it works intimately."

"I was a voyeur, the same as everyone else, sitting on the fringe. It's why I feel guilty." Voicing my concerns hadn't been an option before. "The difference was, I paid attention to the books I read."

"You believe you were a willing participant, the same as the rest?"

"No. I read, unlike the others who skim, review and move on. I error corrected and edited original content—until it wasn't."

"You were choosey then about who they plagiarized?"

"No. Never. I ran with the evidence. I disappeared from their radar the same way you did."

"What evidence did you have to be precise? Their plots?"

"Yes. And they chose to leave them. I'm unsure if they believed their lie–they were *creating*–or that I'd not speak out."

"There's a third option." His words hang in the silence between us.

"I'm well aware. I could have used the plots myself."

"Yet you chose not to. Why?"

"Who would stand up and tell the story? I witnessed readers and authors fold under the pressure of greed and jealousy. They lived their fiction. Became the plastic characters—Barbie dolls or battered women—unloved—transformed into lies and the stories they fake published. "

"We saw so many people who loved them fall. The more attention and devotion, the more they devour and suck dry. They leave desiccated bodies in their wake. If someone can't keep up with the manic pace, they're forced out."

"Reliant upon others for every aspect of the process. Ask yourself then, how were they able to maintain the facade?"

"As one fell silently, another was always ready to take their place. In the way teams sought out manuscripts, ripe for the picking, authors were hunting their next human resource."

"Was any of it real?"

"The source of their words, at some point, perhaps. I'm not certain how far you'd need to go back. 2012 became their set point."

"Who's to say it was their first time round?"

I'd considered this several times. It all started and ended with one account, one date. "It had to be. They refined the process with each new injection of eager sacrifice. Drew in every piece they could find and utilized it until nothing remained."

"Or until too many questions appear."

"The majority of mine was after the fact. Writing reviews, similar plots, and quotes developed between the group. The more we read, the uglier and more complex it became."

"At what point do you cease? When they win the game or fold and walk away?"

"I doubt it will ever be over. In the same way, artificial intelligence will replace predictive text we'll watch them grow and prosper. Those who sat on this—and still sit silently—gained too much. Knowledge, power, cards in the game, if they out the conspiracy, they lose too."

"Won't readers act? Won't they rally and demand a change of direction?"

"How many addicts do you know? It takes strong will and determination to succeed and beat addiction."

"So what happens to Indie?"

"They continue to fester and pick at each other's wounds. The protagonists have called an uneasy truce until book sales slow again."

"I think most have hit their peak."

"Correction, most have run out of raw material and the ability to produce a product without any significant effort on their behalf."

"So now they recycle their own?"

"Or combine teams—co-write—merge two sources, developing a new style."

"I'm not sure they'll make it work."

"Neither am I. The driving force was easy money. Factor in human non-compliance and failure to discover resources we're about to see a drought."

Chapter Twelve

I'd not checked my social media chats following Evie's death. Mid-January, I went in to clear out abandoned groups, and ensure I'd blocked them on every platform.

It appeared Gloria had been persistent, which was sweet–also a little creepy. Discovering her messages couldn't have come at a worse time, we were being attacked from all sides.

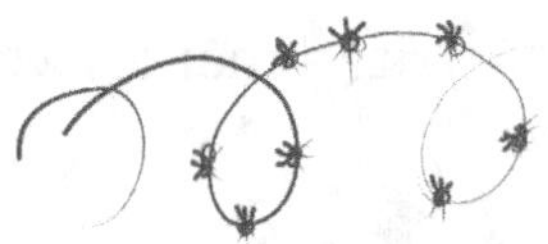

24th December Gloria's_Reading

Gloria: *Hey Kat. I just wanted to see how you're doing. I'm sorry I couldn't get there yesterday. Totally understand if you don't reply to this. I just need you to know I was thinking about you all day. Sending you love xx. Miss your face.*

26th December Gloria's_Reading

Gloria: *Just me again. Hope you found a modicum of pleasure on Christmas Day. Did you catch up with your boys? Was Dale ok, or are the brakes still on with visits? Ours was really quiet. I'm avoiding chat, Dee, Caz, and the whole crazy thing. Let me know if you're alive. Thinking of you. xx*

30th December Gloria's_Reading

Gloria: *Back again. I know you're still hurting and distance is important, but I think you need to see me. Coffee, somewhere safe and public? Name the time and place, I'll be there.*

5th January Gloria's_Reading

Gloria: *I can't begin to imagine what you're going through, Kat. Fuck it's cold today, this climate change is crazy. Yeah, I know, Evie and her whole resetting nature. She's right I think. Hope you have your pumpkin spice stocked and you're hidden away keeping warm. Look, I get you don't want to be around us, I have something you need. You're reading messages, so I know you've been online. Just give me a time and place, and I'll be out of your life again.*

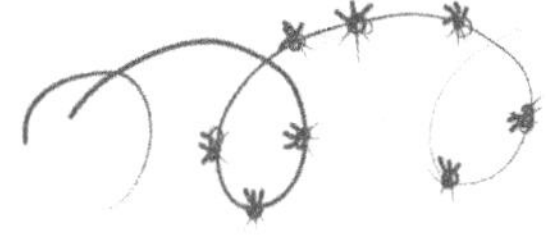

9th January Gloria's_Reading

Gloria: *I have news. Don't want to dump it in here, just in case, you know, maybe you went back. If you did, that's ok. I get it. You'll al-*

ready know I'm blocked everywhere. My authors bailed on me. No one's answering messages. I was kicked from groups anywhere Dee had a foot in. Nothing was said, I'm just banned wherever I look. Even my newsletter signups disappeared. Don't want to pressure you, but I just need a moment.

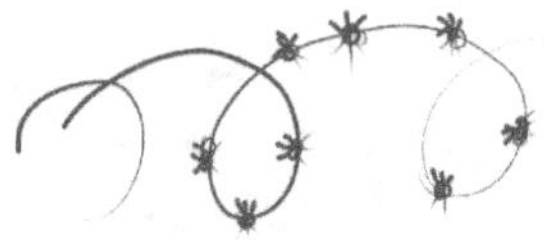

15th January Gloria's_Reading

Gloria: Last chance, Kat. Desi and I are packed. I didn't want to tell you this way, but we're outta here. I'll be at Beanz at 7 p.m. tonight. Our van's loaded, and we'll be leaving from there–if you're not–I'm burning this. Clean start. We're not taking this crap with us—ghosting. Last chance hon. Sorry.

Chapter Thirteen

Jolly Roger Blog
Breaking News!

The Jolly Roger brings you the latest booktok gossip.

Lo and behold the gossipy book factions who believe our banner matches our mission. We are not book pirates.

The scum who inhabit our social media feeds, leeching work, plots, graphics, and imitating ideas—they are the issue.

Wake up Romancelandia! Stop drinking their tainted water and snacking on their laced brownies. Those drugged-up, drunk skanks, need to walk the plank.

If you're with—or use them—you're part of the problem —not the solution.

You've been judged and found guilty by association.

Enjoy the bonfire.

Breaking news!
The Jolly Roger brings you the latest booktok gossip.

Lo and behold the gossipy book factions who believe our banner matches our mission. We are not book pirates.

The scum who inhabit our social media feeds, leeching work, plots, graphics, and imitating ideas—they are the issue.

Wake up Romancelandia! Stop drinking their tainted water and snacking on their laced brownies. Those drugged-up, drunk skanks, need to walk the plank.

If you're with—or use them—you're part of the problem —not the solution.

You've been judged and found guilty by association.

Enjoy the bonfire.

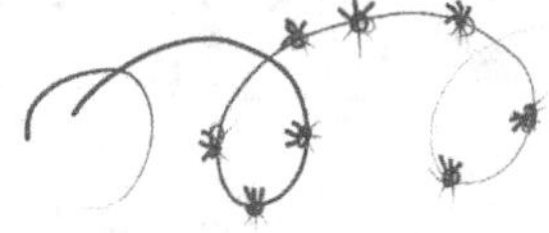

Kat

Past

North Street Beanz, 15th January, 7 p.m

Call me stupid, but I can't resist intrigue. It will cost me dearly one day. The familiar aromas of Beanz hit me as I entered the homey little diner. Pastry, homemade soup, pizza, and their in-house blend, tempt me no end. My stomach gurgles in sympathy. It's been days since I ate a solid meal. Living on caffeine and sugar all week, I'm exhausted.

My order arrives promptly. Dosa and chai tea, paired with a soup of the day. Thanking the waitress, she eyes my combination of carbs with a smirk. "No, it's not a hangover cure."

"No offense, hon, it looks like you've been on a bender." Her snarky response refutes my claim. "Enjoy."

The spicy mulligatawny reminds me of a much-loved comedy episode. Shredded chicken hides within saffron-colored rice. A peppery taste bites in contrast to the smooth texture of the soup. Dipping pieces of dosa, childhood memories flood with endorphins.

Gloria approaches me warily. "Kat, I'm surprised you made it." Taking the seat opposite, she balances, on edge. Ready to take flight, she surveys the room—for whom, I don't know.

"How could I pass up such a gracious invitation, and for what exactly? Another kick in the teeth? A setup?" I know I'm going after the wrong person—but her presence and connections will forever remind me of the team's united front and inaction.

"I don't know who EKS is, but Evie left this with me in case. She was adamant I handed it to you in person, but only if something happened."

"Evie, Kat, and Sara. They were our graduation gifts. Mine's KES. Sara's was SEK. We thought it was cute with all our initials together." I can't believe she kept it.

"As tempting as it was, I didn't open it. It's still sealed the way Evie left it."

I balance the weight of the plastic-wrapped book. Colored tabs protrude from worn pages, and the temptation to rip it open is overwhelming. Turning it over, the spine's cracked, and a page holder ribbon peaks out–frayed and discolored.

"Thank you for keeping this safe, Gloria. I'm sure both Sara and I will gain some comfort from her thoughts."

Chapter Fourteen

"I pose to you, the books you read as a child. How do they compare now, rewritten?" Down to our final discussions for Kat's next novel, I'm attempting to tie up strings.
Following her public fallout and denial by the team, we keep returning to the trending origin of most new material.

"For each fairytale, glittering and fanciful, its source was dark. The originals stand today until a phrase or character's sexuality's questioned. Heaven forbid we break the latest ill-conceived version of history. Imagined slights and *perversions* of those works are now hunted—stripped and buried by a new generation, likened to the Salem Witch Trials." Disgust tinges her voice. "Who taught children to hate with such a veritable passion? What kind of adults will they become running our societies?"

"I'm uncertain. I agree they're not much more than children. They've certainly not been offered any life experience yet. Growing up with technology beyond the imagination of anyone twenty years ago, they appear to learn from it. They're functioning in the same way artificial intelligence does."

"Exactly, they're without compassion or feeling. More machines than human beings. Society's downfall? They embrace a veritable knowledgebase of search engines."

"Pretty much, it seems. Change and growth are healthy. Developing countries must make progress toward economic growth and promote sustainable futures for coming generations."

"I fully support growth. It isn't growth–it's the removal of emotion and humanity. Is this our new reality? Gen Z is canceling history, literature, and culture—whitewashing and cleansing it. The world we envision was predicted by one deemed a crazy messiah and science fiction."

"The same culture strongly supports change, believing this is how history should be perceived."

"Are we using this as our manifesto? To bring society to its knees, returning to the dark ages?"

If I pick up a book from my childhood. Today, the vast difference is heartbreaking. Words are infinite, as are our reading choices. Why must a few continue to repeat our torrid histories? Leave literature alone. Learn from the mistakes and successes of others. Don't attempt to cover Indie's mistakes. Move on.

"Our story of plagiarism and corruption in the book world mimics society. Wake up. Cease. Desist. Art should never be tampered with by anyone other than the artist."

"Do not plagiarize the work of others before you for financial gain. It's not morally justified to just state you need the income. The only way to create hype and market involves a huge outlay or a vast sea of corruption. How can you place your greed above the rights of others? It's a reflection of your twisted mindset and lack of self-love. Consider that."

"We're judged—by everything we do, say, feel, and appear. Our hair, skin, and eye color. Clothing, shoes, monetary value, and status in life. Body image, weight, height, gender, and sexuality. All by society, friends, family, social media, and strangers. The only person entitled to judge is you. The moment we allow others to influence who we are, we lose our identity and our feeling of self-worth. The slippery slope we're heading toward is a one-way trip to endless darkness. The end of who we are, what we know, and how we live."

"View the book world as the glossed-over society we currently inhabit. Love is love. What we love—is not your business."

Change is not necessarily good. History's misinterpretation, based on religion or politics, inevitably leads to war.

Keep your fingers out of the pot, regardless of how tempting another's words are. End the rape and pillage of text, prose, and art—in all its forms.

I know where I'd enjoy seeing book pirates, blog teams, and corrupt authors skulking. No threats, only promises—leave genuine art and the life work of others, *the fuck alone.*

Chapter Fifteen

Present

Damon

J.D. Publishing

"How certain are you that the leaks aren't from within the distributor, Kat?" I wait, watching her chew her bottom lip. The temptation to reach over and run my finger along the seam distracts me from her response. "Sorry, I missed the last part."

"Hmm." Kat's voice drops an octave. "Were you thinking about last night, perhaps?"

"Possibly." I shift position, memories of heat and friction adding to my discomfort. "Leaks." I clear my throat, intent on business. "How many arcs would an average reader pick up in a year?"

"A professional reviewer? Listening in on chats, at two per day, around seven hundred books. Why?"

Fully aware I needed to maintain my own search records, I'd begun verifying the public records Kat implied existed. "I'm looking at a review platform dispensing them like candy. Readers have percentages and rankings against their review accounts."

"I think I know the one. Don't get me started on the pros and cons there. It's a pirate paradise."

"How many of those readers go on to purchase the book on release?"

"Very few. They're not fans, possibly 5% on a good day."

"I came across a bizarre blog story, it wasn't new, but it does explain the free-book mentality. They priced books on release against the same available to arc. Tallied the monthly cost, and declared their reads as savings." Why an author wasn't paying attention to these claims was a bigger surprise. If they can afford to lose so much, I dread to think what they're pulling in.

"You've got to be kidding? What about the author? How do they factor into it?"

Kat pulls up her phone and begins tallying figures. "Think numbers, as always. If you allocate two hundred ARCS, even at a reduced release day price of $5.99, it doesn't sound much. If a reader picks up a book a day, one hundred and eighty dollars per month in sales are lost. If they're grabbing two or three, and some do, there's no telling where it ends. This is one review platform alone. If it's two, there go four hundred lost purchases, and so on."

"So potentially a big name, with on-release books sale offers at $5.99, with an easy one thousand dollars value in ARCs." I'd already assumed this, with an added zero.

"They're losing tens of thousands a year, which equates to buying those reviews." Again her disdain for blogger behavior, reminds me she's on the right side of this fight, thank God. "Don't forget how many of the review copies are on-sold to pirate sites or cataloged on request blogs. There's the possibility of sales. Last time I checked, they're clearing twenty-five to sixty dollars, per book. With platform technology changing, try the upper limits now." I watch as the numbers transfer to her notebook, rising higher with each pen stroke.

"You'd assume authors would reduce early access then? Cut losses and protect?"

Kat's hair tie fly's free, sliding to the floor, as she rakes her fingers through the length, twisting it up into a bun. Sliding the pencil in, and securing it, she goes back to her manic note-taking. "Hell no. If it means bragging about a category banner, they'd sell their firstborn. One went as far as publicly stating *'at least someone's reading my books.'* Damn shame the content wasn't hers to begin with."

"Explains the attitude then. They're making bank on something of no personal value to them."

"It's something to consider when you find yourself viewing page after page of pirate access sites, and no takedown notices."

"You're pointing out the obvious - the work's not theirs."

"So, we return to the unpopular opinion, but it's the early reads. To avoid piracy you need to cease early digital copies."

"And rectify the terms of use they breach."

"It's been my stance. Don't forget, inner sanctum expertise." A knowing grin flashes across her face.

"You've proven this repeatedly. Break it down for me. What's in it for the blogger faction to betray their sources?"

"Again, like a broken record, I don't believe it's betrayal when their sources are the plagiarizing bastards, to begin with." Kat digs through the carryall beside her. Popping back up with a smirk. "Found her."

A journal materializes, grasped in her hand, and she deftly flicks through the pages. The worn, tattered leather corners show their age and overuse. With faint gold embossing, the red cover leaks through indistinguishable initials. "My own little Bible. Want to know what she contains, Damon?"

Her honest, open thoughts and secrets? The sanctum's cause and effect—their gamebook?"

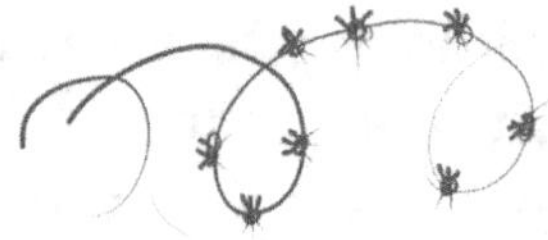

Kat

Absently tracing the worn KEC, I second-guess myself. Sharing this last piece with Damon means we're nearing the end of our journey. Once it's combined with its partner in crime, we have finished. Tucked away–my last weapon had arrived in the form of Evie's notebook.

"If you're not ready, Kat, it can wait."

Shaking my head, Damon's proven his loyalty every step of the way. "You may borrow this while I'm here. No comment, no questions. You have," I check my watch, "an hour." Cautiously I hand my get-out-of-jail-free card to him. "Only an hour. I'll be back."

Chapter Sixteen

Evie

The red book

This book belongs to the amazingly talented
Elizabeth
Love always. Kat and Sara.

If you're reading this, well, I sound like a soppy romance novel. But seriously, if you are, you need to be restrained and sensible about how you use the information within.

I'm serious, Kat. I know how reactionary you are right now.

Sara, the other half of my soul. Words aren't enough, but please know, I'm sorry it led to this.

I did this for us, for everyone we love. For the craft.

EKS forever.

Never forget me. E xx

January 2019

Lessons learned last year:

1. *Never trust what you read is real.*
2. *Plots are recycled and sold.*
3. *Promo covers it all up.*

Dear Diary,

Yeah, I sound like a love-sick teen. This is my last will and testament —joking guys!

I met an amazing team today. Browsing through groups, I won a give-away. Next minute I'm invited to their blogger chat.

These girls are from all over. Ireland, Canada, tiny little Cotswolds, I think one called them. Predominantly from the US, they feel like home.

I'm so excited to fill Kat in. The opportunities are beyond cool. Can I have a girl crush on strangers already lol?

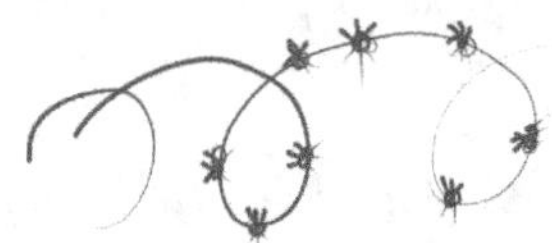

January 12th

Me again. Wow, you'd never believe who dropped into the group today, none other than Drea Dark. She's really cool, funny, and not condescending at all. They bitch about her all over, yet she's sweet-as.

We chatted for hours.

Dee dropped a heap of freebie reads for all of us. Most are new releases, so a penny is saved and all that. All I have to do is drop reviews for them, I get to keep the books. Not like the ARCs we delete after reading. Gotta keep those devices empty, as Dee says.

January 29th

OMFG!!! I woke up this morning, put the coffee on, and checked my emails. Drea's sent me a few signed books as a thank you. She says they'll take a few days, international post is slow, but signed physical books! How cool, and for just a couple of five-star reviews. Easy, peasy.

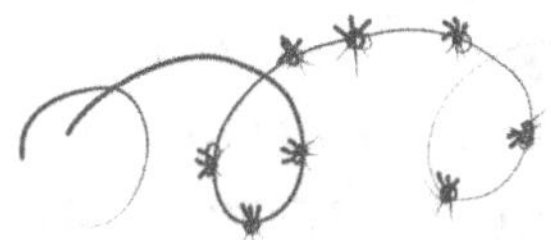

February 9th

Dee's a bitch and a half when you forget to drop her Monday promo. I'm thinking I need a new account, just for my book porn. Some of it's too risqué for Kat's kids to see, she'd kill me for corrupting them.

These guys are genuine though. Polished graphics, and cool pre-set posts. Dee knows how to run a tight team. I kinda hate her most days, but LB says to stay on her good side and 'she'll be right, mate." Aussies are weird. Her accent makes no sense at all. I guess mine doesn't to her either.

February 14th

Happy V-Day to me. The fluffy crap released today is gross, with a capital G. We had to pick three from Dee's post to read, minimum. The first I grabbed, yeah pass. DNF. Dee lost her shit, usual 'she's a best-seller, say thank you and just review'.

She creeps me out some days. I know she has a job to do, but the crap pushed is teenage high school drama. I swear these authors wrote it at fourteen. Repeated storylines, over and over, it's weird. The plots feel *off, but what would I know?*

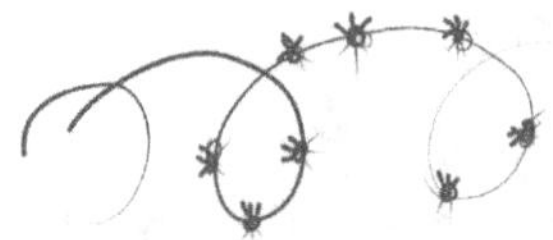

March 9th

So much for maintaining an accurate reading record. I'm flooded with ARCs. I swear I'm reading five hours a day minimum.

At 2 a.m. I'm checking feeds. Some fruit cake is ranting about banned books. Love that word, fruit cake. The girls from the UK call things weird names. I had to remember what Dee wanted us to do. I can't stand her writing style, but you know, to each their own, the team has to jump in and support these people. I dropped a cool quote from her book with Dee's promo posts and bailed.

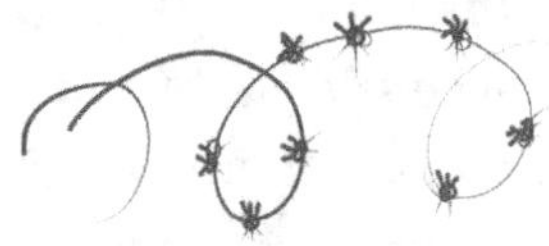

March 21st

Shit another month's almost over and I'm over the drama and information overload. I'm gonna give up trying to keep up with this note idea. I started taking screenshots today. Easier to remember and I can just print them off and stick them in here.

Today's Romancelandia was kinky. Something about vaults and crap. I'm too scared to ask in chat. The last question, Gloria was so rude, I didn't know where to hide.

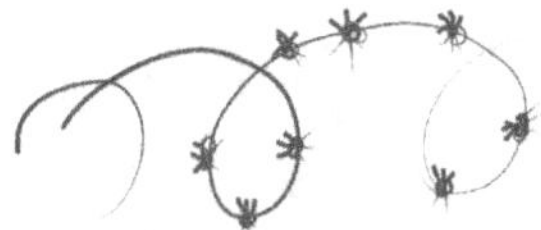

March 30th,

Yeah, something is up. I opened one of Liz Roa's books today and the prologue was familiar. This young girl was kidnapped, she's some kind of mafia princess. The motorcycle club saved her. I love it, but it's like Drea's book from last month. Weird, hey?

The team's nervous on this one. We're keeping teasers brief. Reviews have to be vague. Dropped within 24 hours of receipt. Pushy much?

Twists and turns, God I hate those phrases. I'm kinda sick of being told what to say.

Dee wants me to set up another review account. I don't know. It's kinda dishonest, but they all do it, so. I should ask Kat what she thinks, but I know the answer before I even finish. She'd be pissed off and tell me no.

Saw this in my feed today, so I grabbed a SS. Don't know the author, but the cover's the same as Lacey's. Can they do it? Aren't there rules or something?

April 1st

Dee carried on about this new social media platform and included book stacks. I don't own most of the arcs I've read. The physical copies she promises haven't arrived. Easy out, blaming the postal service.

The deal is bloggers can cut and paste the cover photo in. Drea told us to print off her covers, the same size as a book on our shelves. Just wrap the paper around, and tada, we have a photo-ready copy.

I can't bring myself to try it, talk about being dishonest. So, I zoom into a few big blogger accounts, the ones with ten thousand followers, and a few hundred in return. The pretty color-coded feeds. I swear every second book is fake. I know, because the gloss covers are flat in photos. These guys aren't readers, they're ads.

April 16th

Yes!!! I won a box in the huge local publishing group today. Influencer pack, exclusive covers, and a few digital flat-lay photo backdrops. The one-offs cost a shit load. I looked at a few on Zan's page, the cheap crap most use. PMSL. The pens are bigger than books and the outline of the book covers in hands. OMFG, their nails change daily. Edited and photoshopped inserts are hilarious. Crap, reminder, don't tell her how cheap they look with wooden macrame beads, rope, and paper. Did they all shop at a dollar store?

Now I just need to work out how to superimpose my real books into their fake photos. Dee said it's a no-brainer, she'll help me. One condition, I need to get Kat into the chat. I might have dumped her in it as an editor, Dee said there are a few more freebies if I can get her to help out for a while.

I don't know. She's not going to get on with Gloria or Dee.

Kat will kill me if she finds out.

16th December

Dear Kat,

I swapped mediums, I didn't want to contaminate this further. When you receive this, you know where my backups are. Please don't let Sara read them until you're done.

xxx

Chapter Seventeen

Present

Damon

Evie's ramblings were kind of cute, Kat did say she was extremely naïve in the beginning. The little pieces here and there added up to more than they'd considered.

More fool the Smut Mafia, sweet little Evie wasn't as ignorant as they'd assumed. They'd let a lion cub into their den. If the hints so far have any foundation, she grew up to be a lioness.

Stretching my cramped fingers, my mind drifted to Kat reading this. A voice from the dead, recounting her time in the group and her last months. It only adds more heartbreak. Their investigation needs to be put to rest.

Kat's dump and run, finding something to occupy herself, was a bad omen.

My phone buzzed across my desk. Nadine and her duty of care for her favorite client, my mother hen, was in full force today.

"Found her, Damon. She's downstairs browsing advertising and upcoming review options. Do you want me to offer her something, or leave her alone?" Nadine's voice vibrated with built-up tension. Her attempts at supporting Kat previously were brushed off. Maybe this time, a distraction will help.

"John has a few spare copies of the new SWF novel down there. Try offering her one. It's right up her alley. From memory, Jane missed a few points in editing. See if it tempts her."

"On it boss. I thought Aramoyr might be her style too. I'll see if she's interested. Anything else, in case she dislikes the synopsis?"

"Norm Zander's splatter-kink was a fun read. Sign out the three and set her up next to mine. Try tempting her with…"

"Your pumpkin spice, I know. I sent Fiona down for pastries and something light for lunch. I'll be back in the office in a few."

"Thanks, Nadine, you're a doll."

"And if I wasn't happily married for twenty-five years, I'd be taking you up on your suave offers." The lilt of her voice broadens, and her Scottish descent shines through.

"I don't know what I'd do without you."

"Yes, you do. You'd have that hot clerk from payroll here seeing to your every whim."

"Workplace harassment and intimidation aside, he is hot. Wonder if he swings both ways?"

"Damon D! Too much information. You might want to check out things with Kat first."

Choking back a laugh, there's no pulling the wool over Nadine's eyes. "Yes ma'am. I'll be right on it as soon as I line up some body armor, just in case. Gotta protect the crown jewels, you know."

I flip open the first of three numbered journals. Propping my feet on my desk, I settle in, delving into erratic and desperate ravings, as Evie began her spiral.

Chapter Eighteen

Damon

My hour with Evie's books stretched into three. Storm-front Kat, blasted through my door, throwing the SWF copy on my desk.

"Do you truly comprehend the meaning of pitch black? Not the twisted mind fuckery of blended words—stolen from the greats. Real creators, words that hit hard, with a consuming need to speak their character's truth."

"I'm assuming you don't approve then?" I wave at the offending copy.

Kat's abrupt entrance is a welcome relief. Sequestered alone next door, she'd been too quiet all afternoon.

"Pitch is an art form. The author must delve into the recesses of the human mind and live within, as they write their story. Not clinically from the outside, but a true mind and body meld. A psychological connection between the character and the author."

"Jekyll and Hyde style? Two voices, one physical body?"

"To write effectively, yes. Research only goes so far. The voices creating a book feel they're living beings. Imagine the horror of visiting the inner workings of a sociopathic mind. Take it multiple steps further, and delve into a psychopath or a true split personality disorder.”

“The sterile observation style seems to be the preferred method.”

“Have you read an honest-to-God, pitch-black romance novel?”

“My thoughts on romance tend to oppose yours, so no.”

“I’m going to recommend a few books by their designated vault authors. Don’t judge, just read. Come back when you’ve completed the task, and tell me why you don’t enjoy romance again.”

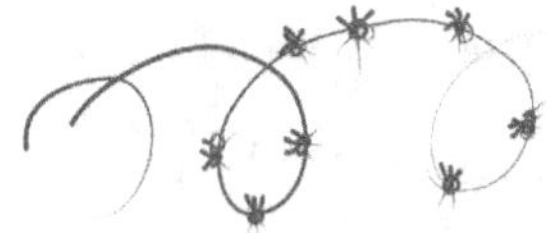

Damon

I stopped by the local hole-in-the-wall bookstore after work. Browsing shelves, I discovered the authors Kat recommended. Doorstop weight books lined the shelves, front and center, perfect black shadows, in a sea of color. Impressive in their simplicity and original design, I browsed titles.

Intrigued by a synopsis, I added a few more to my basket. Thank goodness for tax write-offs. If they’re not as enthralling as she seems to feel they are, I’ll not tell Kat I added extras.

By three a.m. I was addicted to the melodic prose of her favorite finds. A sonata didn’t begin to describe the mood or words, as they ran across the pages.

I could feel the heat, and smell the deep, luminous pools of water, as they built breathtaking scenery. Hints of faraway places, diverse relationships, and interconnected, ongoing storylines, engaged me like no other.

Sleep was something I'd willingly lose, replaced by a world of intrigue, and pure romance.

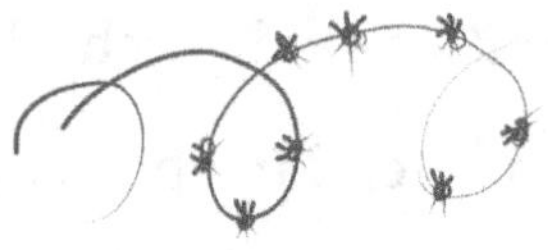

Damon
6:30 a.m.

Damon: Kat, she's a genius. Where the hell did you find her?

Kat: You do know what time it is Damon, don't you?

Damon: Sure do. I've been up all night testing your secret weapon. Whose pen name is it? I can't see them hidden unless it's intentional.

Kat: Your turn to play amateur sleuth. I'll meet you in an hour for breakfast. Bring your A-game, and who you think it is.

Damon: Can I interest you in breakfast here?

Kat: Sorry, no can do. I have a date at 9:30 with another guy.

Damon: …

Kat: Joking about the other guy, but I do have a prior arrangement.

Damon: I'll see you at our usual, in an hour then.

Chapter Nineteen

Present

Damon

North Street Beanz, 7:45 a.m.

Nothing new, Kat was running late. I placed our order on arrival and went through the plethora of unattended emails in my inbox.

"Morning, handsome." Kat slid in opposite, fresh-faced, with her usual haphazard clothing choice. Her green dress conflicted with the pink cardigan and the odd rusty brown color through her hair.

"Tell me how *that* happened," I swear if I laugh, she'd strike me. "This will be entertaining."

"Research, I don't know." Flicking hair from her face, she wraps a tie around the length, pulling it back. "I forgot it was in, and it didn't quite work out." The grin doesn't leave her face. "So, what's our early morning catch-up over?"

"Haven't you worked it out yet?"

She almost jumps across the table in her eagerness. "You read them? Tell me you didn't stay up all night reading *romance*?"

"I did, and yes, most of the night." Her mood is contagious, I'm happy to share my thoughts, and she deserves the recognition. "It feels familiar."

"But she's no one."

Our breakfast arrives, and Kat sets to pulling apart her pastry. "Give, Damon. What did you think?"

"In one word, classy. The word flow, structure, plot, and character arc all gel perfectly. Possibly some of the best I've read."

I swear I've made her year, the pleasure of acknowledging one book by her favorite author, she'll never let it go if she knows I purchased the entire back catalog online.

"I can pick them, right? You really enjoyed it?"

Unable to keep a simple secret, she'll hold this one over me indefinitely. "I enjoyed two."

Kat chokes on her latte. "Two? By the same *romance* author?" She peers under the tablecloth, "what did you do with Damon, the big publishing executive?"

"I read two of your recommendations." The grin cracking her face grows wider. "Enjoyed one more than the other, and possibly ordered the back catalog." This I'll never live down.

"Debate it then. You've read it, she's the source. The top of the Dolly Varden cake."

"A what cake? Our conversations are bizarre, but baking references are foreign to me, Kat."

"It's the ultimate princess cake for kids. Think of a Barbie doll wedged in a domed cake, and dressed in frosting for her ball gown." Pulling herself up, her eyebrow quirks at my ignorance." Surely you remember those gaudy cakes, at kids' parties?"

All I can do is nod before we head down a cooking path again.

"You believe she's a word source?"

"Based on the plot and a few quotes, she's one of the dozens they're ripping from."

"Why? This is the part I don't understand. It makes sense, reading through the rest. Plots could be pulled from one book, broken down to six or more, with ease." Winding up for what's undoubtedly a big reveal, I'm hit by a name from the past. "I think she's Alexandria, aka Jada River. Do you remember her thrillers around 2010 to 2012?"

"I do remember the name, Evie and I loved her work. They referred to her as the pretty girl who sat in the corner at signings. A little awkward, and ignored. Didn't they say she was too smart for publishing?"

Kat's bangs fall over her eyes as she nods in agreement. "I think I'm close. I found an old out-of-focus signing from a 2008 event. She was straight out of college, a protégé already."

"Regardless of her identity, why choose her work?"

"To the mean girls, this is payback. If you don't fold your hand and surrender, they take what they want."

Chapter Twenty

Jolly Roger Blog
Breaking News!

The Jolly Roger brings you the latest booktok gossip.

Online influencers are falling like flies.
Checking just a few hashtags on booktok will direct you to
book services spamming feeds with ads via advanced
reader copy signups.

You do realize, authors pay for services, instead of
running online ads? They push you, the reader, to avoid
their accounts being banned. You're the ones breaching
terms of use for social media.

There are hundreds of businesses established under
independent publishing. The readers sharing are not
necessarily paid, they often receive early book copies for
review or promotion.

None of you state it's advertising. It's not like you're
buying physical books.

None of you declare you are influencers.

We. See. You.

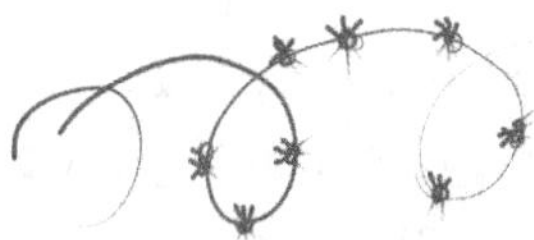

Unpopular opinion, but the legal terms of use are breached repeatedly by authors circumnavigating every possible rule. I understood the social media warnings. I don't think many did. It was anticipated to roll through quietly, but nothing's gone smoothly in recent years.

The dictionary defines exclusivity as a contract that specifies the exclusiveness of the right.

Hand out before a release via any means removes the exclusive nature of the product. I'd be pissed off if something claimed exclusivity and multiple people received it too.

The same applies to physical book editions. Long waitlists and unicorn copies—pretty shiny things used to entice the desperate.

Common sense and accountability are lacking. The usual culprits won't change their spots, just their pen names. As fast as they release, they've ghosted again. Watch the cycle and consider the numbers—always the numbers. They don't lie, but the players do with their contrived games.

One piece of the scam we'll always return to–processes. The removal of books is not an issue created by the distributor. It's the raw files provided by the author or publisher. Categories are selected, and an over eighteen box is ticked by the honest. Providing a copy in any form before release–equates to a breach of an exclusive contract. Simple. It's publicly available and searchable information.

While I feel for anyone hit by piracy, the problem does not reside with the platforms. It's the author's method to gain reviews for their book pre-release.

Nondisclosure agreements do not exist. The generic 'do not share' in a sign-up? It's all a farce. Pirate sites hold unreleased books prior—always. They're readily available, formatted versions. So where did they originate?

Rather than abusing a system in place, allowing everyone to publish for no upfront cost, assume responsibility for actions that create piracy via arcs.

Why won't people read terms of use? Change is coming, so check the fine points. Readers and authors need to understand the risks they're under and the drama they've created, not the platforms.

Chapter Twenty-one

Kat

If I were to look up deception in a dictionary, I'd need to start at the back under Z.

How did I not connect the dots? The path I was led down, the hints, connections, all came from one source. The driving force had the most to gain, and even more to lose. Her history was shrouded in mystery.

We paid close attention to Evie for years, and forgot, Zan was there beside us, learning what made each of us tick—our hopes, vanities, and desires.

Zan's story's not mine to tell. Suffice it to say, she instigated a new wave of noise against the corrupt, in defense of her own words. In doing so, in pushing both Evie and myself, unknowing she was close to home—someone we admired, and loved deeply—and she cost Evie her life.

They play for keeps. They don't back down. They do not bend or break–Zan taught us that.

Zan's disclosure before I confronted her, freed me from the pain of betrayal. It doesn't make it any easier, though Sara will be able to move on with her life, and their child when she arrives.

Her deceit drove a wedge between all of us. I'd like to think it's repairable with Damon, but I'm dubious. Sara and I lost Evie, while Zan continued her grand experiment. The cold hard bitch, I still can't fathom how she escaped detection for so long. While she attempted to unseat the reigning Indie royalty and take back her own words, she lost so much more. She chose her path, if she'd come clean from the start, perhaps Evie may have survived the skirmish, if not the war.

We need to learn to either move on and distance ourselves from them or stay in a hole. They'll bury us time and time again if we let them. In Zan's case, this wasn't her first time around, it wouldn't be her last.

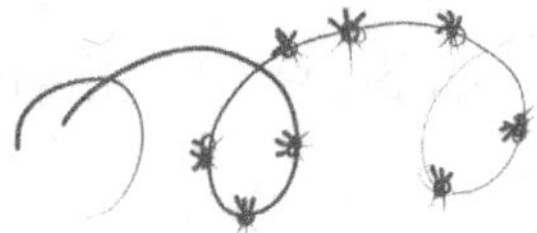

Uninvited, I let myself into Damon's office and took up residence in my favorite spot. I knew I wouldn't wait long for his arrival. I did achieve a morning's work by the time he breezed in, my laptop was already loaded with links ready to go live. Checking his schedule, his morning was clear from 10 onwards. He arrived at 10:10 promptly, with coffee and a brown paper bag of something warm and tantalizing. He dropped it on his desk. "I was surprised to find you here, Kat."

"I can't even sneak into your office without her discovering me." I should be angry, but Damon's knowing I was here, meant he was willing to hear me out.

Be part of the solution, not the problem. I've cleaned my page of those I don't interact with, or know personally. The same goes for groups, and pages, and I've certainly blocked some of those proven to do wrong.

"With the dam emptied, you don't need to put your finger back in, Damon." He stills, dropping his pen, and it rolls gently across the desk. "Pretend everything's fine—or, we can wait until it's overflowing again."

His hesitation says more than any words will. "At what point in our acquaintance did you discover my involvement? On second thought, don't answer, I'm probably better off not knowing."

"I'm happy to enlighten you when you dropped the ball—but we both know you didn't do it by accident. You required a willing partner, and I needed a new mission."

"I thought I was being subtle, so much for my charisma winning you over." His chuckle eases the tension, and my concern we were over.

"Initially, we both had ulterior motives." I watch the finger tap the edge of his chin, considering my next response. "Don't worry, Damon, I'm not going anywhere. Our reasons may have differed, but the outcome remains the same."

"It began as a game. You needed assistance. I was able to facilitate it. Your voice was heard, it made a difference for a few."

"I'm not willing to accept it was only a few, Damon. They heard, like every other threat, they ignored and buried the content—the bodies."

"You need to understand, this is how Indie survives. It's the only way they know."

"Is survival enough? I don't think so anymore. Indie was beautiful. Before the games, before the world changed. We had a voice for good, a sense of purpose. From talented people like yourself, we encouraged change and acceptance."

"Without a Queen to adore and undermine, they have no purpose now. No drive to succeed. Most remain average, at best. They'll settle back into the mundane routine they knew before. Their actions are exposed until someone develops a new scenario to beat the system."

"Not good enough. There has to be a better way. What was the purpose behind this skirmish, if we were destined to lose and repeat history?"

"As with any war, it's the only way we know how to play the game. Expose, clean house, and as Dee said, rip, rinse, repeat."

"I have a better idea. Game over."

I open my laptop and hit enter, watching the upload percentage rise. "Website's done, research has been uploaded. Links to every known site, blog, and author involved—device and home addresses, went wide. There's nothing they can do about it now." Flicking the power switch beside me, my hard drive's about to be toast. "Sorry, Damon. No more."

"Do you honestly believe this is it—there's no backup?"

"I made sure of it this time. They're done."

Epilogue

Every single file we read is digitally traced. Have you considered how often you copy text, screenshots, or download a recipe? When you grab a book review online, a sample, borrow or purchase, your movements are traced. Heaven forbid you see no harm in piracy. The thing is, the moment you open the file, big brother knows. Your service provider, the point of sale —your device. The moment it's loaded for reading—other than breaking multiple federal laws—you have been marked. Unlike a stacked deck or marked notes, the indelible ink is not washed off, no matter how many times you attempt to rinse.

The next time you spend your hard-earned money and the cashier short changes you; perhaps you notice, but more often you don't until it's too late. Don't bemoan how you've been ripped off, how you had to work hard for your money if you're guilty even of one book, in this big picture.

This little parody was split into multiple parts, purely to prove a point. It wasn't shared before the release. It wasn't nor will it be, sent out as digital gifts, breaching terms of service.

It's gone straight from the source to publication.

The error is not within the system. The issue is within the community. It's not the damn hard-working people who think they've failed—they haven't—their words are broken down by groups who believe they're invisible. Wrong book this time guys.

It's not the fault of artists who work for a few dollars an hour. The error lies entirely with those who lack the moral fiber and basic human decency to treat others as they'd like to be treated themselves. How would you like a few kicks to the ribs while you're down? While you're shaming a reading choice, hunting to plagiarize the minute their back is turned.

Indie needs to take a damn hard look at every aspect. From original concept notes, proof of who is responsible for what's uploaded. Registering publications, copyright, topography, the list is endless. This is a business venture after all. It is not a hobby if money is exchanged.

This is our community:
The bloggers who hold not one, not two, but five-plus accounts offer fake reviews.
The promotional companies know they do, support the idea, and are fully aware their readers pirate pre-releases.
The authors review their own work.
The editors, alpha and beta readers review, without clearly stating such.
The ability to review without purchase is a privilege they abuse.

In what world do we live that this situation is ok? For every positive unverified, there are multiple negative unverified reviews, loaded by the same trolls stealing content. It takes little research to seek out the pond scum who feel not only entitled, but justified in doing so.

Ask about characters, ideas, and thought processes. When an author is unable to remember a character, a timeframe, or an event, ask why. Search for those book groups selling plots and the vast number of authors you read who reside there. Many have from their pen name's inception.

Consider this little parody fictional, but take a closer look. Pull back the veil, and pay attention to the sheep cloning each other. Writing requires research, and everyone knows, there must be factual elements involved for it to be believable.

Search for truth in literature. Don't settle for second best and pay those who steal words time and time again. When they're caught out, they'll cry wolf, claim innocence, and reinvent. Check those long abandoned pen names. Ones who are no longer published. Ask why? Are they backups for reinvention purposes, did they retire, or are they part of the plagiarism scams occurring right under your noses?

When a reader or author states their story is not literature, creating a negative and derogatory image of the romance genre–step the hell away from them. Words hold great power. Demeaning an art form, for a dollar, send them to the vaults where they belong.

Zan's story wasn't mine to tell. Maybe you'll find an extended epilogue from her later on. Or, perhaps she'll keep her secrets in her own red book.

Glossary

A brief list of terminology has been included for quick reference. If you are unfamiliar with any term, research is golden when reading. The new generation of readers learn everything from social media, and quite often, don't actually read the books in front of them. If they did, we would not be here.

Readers overall are intelligent—to assume otherwise, is vanity—never underestimate a reader. This is a key only, not a detailed or technical outline. The lookup option in the ebook feature connects to both internet search and dictionaries. It's a tool too often forgotten. Some readers may be less familiar with the included abbreviations.

Glossary of terms for the current generation.

This is a quick lingo decoder—not fluff or a page scam. Newbies slurp social slop, skip real reads. If they cracked spines, this mess wouldn't exist, right? Readers, they're razor-sharp—underrate 'em, regret it.

- •. Ebook lookup: Web/dict ninja tool, dust it off.
- • Indie: Self-pub mavericks or their word dumps.
- • CMOS: Chicago Manual of Style—editors' sacred scroll for grammar, comp, rules.
- • Content Warning: Author's red flag for gut-twisters. (Scrap "TW"—triggers are quirky, like clown terror.)

- NDA: Gag order.
- ARC: Pre-release tease.
- Street Team: Author's cheer mob for drop days.
- Boost Group: Comment conga line to hack algos (boomerangs bad).
- Wishlist: Amazon beg list—books for pity buys.
- ROAK: Surprise swag from public begs.
- Alpha Reader: Plot surgeon—big pic, chars, glue; edit-savvy pal.
- Beta Reader: Chapter sniper—flow fouls, glitches; NDA if not ride-or-die.
- ARC Reader: Hype drone for buffed drafts—not edit fodder.
- Word Choice: Ditch duds for dazzlers.
- Repetition: Loop killers—words on repeat? Axe 'em.
- Copy Editor: Word wizard—sharpens scribbles.
- Developmental Editor: Structure slayer—plot, build fixes.
- Line Editor: Dev mongrel.
- Proofreader: Typo terminator—no chit-chat.
- Editorial Assessment: MS takedown—style, speed, wins/losses.
- Pass: Edit circuit.
- MS: Raw word beast.
- Promo: Plug-and-play ads/graphics; stock pics shield sharers' hides.
- Annotations: Scribbles/highlights; now TikTok tease bait.
- Genre: Lit bin, e.g., romance.
- Trope: Genre spice, e.g., rom-suspense.
- Smut: Plot? Pfft—all bang.
- Spice: Steam gauge, hot as hell.
- Blurb: A snappy book tease—back-cover bait to hook suckers.
- Sock Puppet: Fake accounts puppeteered by authors for self-praise or rival sabotage.
- Plagiarism: Word theft—lifting plots, lines, or whole chunks without credit. Indie plague.
- Ghostwriter: Shadow scribe churning out "your" book for cash; credit? Optional.
- Review Bombing: Mob assault via fake low stars to tank a rival's rank.
- Ebook Scam: Free library hustle—page-stuffing or bot-reads for payout cheats.
- Booktok: TikTok's romance circus—hype machine for viral smut,

often scripted.

• ARC Farm: Shady reviewer mills churning canned praise for promo perks.

• Gate (e.g., #Gate): Scandal suffix—publishing drama exposed, then buried.

• Black Hat Promo: Dirty tricks to game algos—fake engagement, bought buzz.

For those who speak traditionally acknowledged English:

•. Indie: Independently published/author.

• CMOS: The Chicago Manual of Style—editing/grammar bible.

• Content Warning: Author's alert for potential triggers. (Not "TW"—triggers are personal, e.g., clowns.)

• NDA: Non-disclosure agreement.

• ARC: Advanced reader copy.

• Street Team: Author-specific promo readers for releases.

• Boost Group: Group commenting to game algorithms (often counter productive).

• Wishlist: Amazon list of items (books) for gifting.

• ROAK: Random act of kindness—gift from public wishlist.

• Alpha Reader: Oversees development (plot, character); trusted editor-friend.

• Beta Reader: Chapter feedback on flow/inconsistencies; trusted/NDA.

• ARC Reader: Promo reviewer of polished book; not editor.

• Word Choice: Optimal terminology/synonyms.

• Repetition: Overused words/phrases.

• Copy Editor: Sharpens wording.

• Developmental Editor: Feedback on plot/build/structure.

• Line Editor: Hybrid developmental.

• Proofreader: Final typo hunt; no feedback.

• Editorial Assessment: Overall manuscript review (style, pace, issues).

• Pass: Editing read-through.

• MS: Manuscript/raw book.

• Promo: Pre-made posts/graphics for sharing (licensed photos indemnify sharers).

• Annotations: Notes/highlights; now social media hype tool.

- Genre: Literature category, e.g., romance.
- Trope: Subcategory, e.g., romantic suspense.
- Smut: Plotless sex.
- Spice: Sexual tension/heat level.

About the author

Evie is the pen name of a writer who knows better than to enter the insane arena of independent publishing. The brainchild of a dare, clicking upload was possibly the strangest thing she's ever contemplated.

Trained in many things, master of none, now a stay at home fur mother, volunteer and avid reader.

Of the belief you're best suited to write what you know, it's what she was taught, after all, Evie first published as a student. Co-writing articles over the years, her shelves remain full of untold stories.

Reprieve (omnibus, includes additional scenes)

The Algal Bloom: fact, fiction or conspiracy.

Coming soon: Cry Wolf

Review Journals, notebooks and autograph books available on Amazon.

A SINGLE DAD AND A BACHELOR AUCTION
—WHAT COULD POSSIBLY GO WRONG?
Locked & Loaded
GENEVIEVE L. HUGHES
REPRIEVE BOOK 1

Preview: Locked & Loaded

Dale

I lost a bet. In typical sibling rivalry fashion, I now owed my sister a favor. Little did I anticipate she'd hold me to it and cash in said debt.

Stripped down, parading my wares—I'm dressed as a cowboy at a charity auction. Never let it be said a Reid reneges on his word.

Deflowering an exquisite beauty, was not on the agenda.

Belle

Falling for a single dad was never my intent. A quick fling, a one-night stand, and bye-bye to my v-card was all I wanted.

Who'd have thought a daddy figure was my kind of kink?

Locked and loaded, a masked cowboy stole my fragile heart.

Prologue

Dale

I watch my phone dance across the highly polished desk. I ignore my sister Kaye for the third time. A call on a Friday night from my matchmaking twin never bodes well. I should be thankful it isn't Mom checking in on me now Bobby's in college. Empty nest syndrome is real. I miss the boys and the disruption they caused.

As I close my laptop, the doorbell chimes through the hollow entryway. Bare hardwood floors remind me of my divorce and Kat's absence. Maybe Kaye's right. It's time to put myself back on the market. Kat and I were childhood sweethearts, married too young to survive the drama life throws at you. Including my already limited social life, I was left to raise the boys when she walked out. Dating hasn't been the top of my priorities.

The bell rings again, ignoring the notification on my phone. Whoever's there is damn persistent.

I swing open the door, ready to drive off any unsolicited sales spiel for random things we don't need.

"About time little brother," Kaye breezes in uninvited. "Grab whatever, we're heading out."

A quick check of my gray sweatpants and hole-ridden gym tee doesn't suggest a night on the town in anyone's books.

"Pass. It's been a long week. I'll settle in with takeout and a beer. You're welcome to stay, of course."

"Nope, not happening, Kiddo. We," she waves between us, "are heading out for a much-needed bonding session."

"I'm positive we," I mimic her conductor's move, "bond enough through work, Sis. Pizza and a movie sound more like my kind of deal. You know it's been a long week, but thanks anyway."

Kaye grabs my elbow and points me toward the stairs. "You have ten minutes, Dale. Enough brooding. It's time to get you back on the horse."

I groan inwardly at her favorite reference. Cowboys appear to be the trend at work. The cheesy innuendos run rampant, as do our dress code these days. Her boots tap out a staccato, and I know I don't stand a chance against her in this mood.

"Fine. Give me ten, I'll tidy up." I look Kaye up and down. "Smart casual is fine, I assume?"

With a light shove forward, Kaye's pleasure is evident. "Keep it simple and comfortable. Jeans and those sexy boots the girls love. I have the perfect spot booked."

My sister's idea of perfection and mine are two entirely different things. "Based on your shoes...at least it won't be rock climbing again."

"Stop wasting time, we'll be late."

Casual, it is then. I'm on the losing side regardless once she's set her mind to something.

Social media links

https://linktr.ee/glh_books